PRAISE FOR *MESSY*

D1636264

"Feel good again! Robin brings to life the reality that joy is within reach, regardless of where you are in the moment."

—***Garry Ridge,*** *chairman emeritus of WD-40 Company*

"Robin Shear nails this often-misunderstood topic of joy. I'm certain readers will be 'Robinized' by her practical insight and wisdom throughout."

—***Kurt A. David,*** *Emmy Award–winning executive producer and TV host, majority owner of Glory Days Productions, international speaker on change management, and cofounder and chairman of PurposePoint*

"I could not put this book down! If you have an imperfect life (because who doesn't?!), read *Messy Joy* and start feeling good now. Robin's joy is contagious."

—***Kim Walsh Phillips,*** *founder of Powerful Professionals Business Coaching and coauthor of No B.S. Guide to Direct Response Social Media Marketing*

"I have been speaking and writing for years about joy in the context of our work lives and really appreciate how Robin shares solid strategies for adding it to everyday life—no matter how challenging. I loved reading *Messy Joy!*"

—***Richard Sheridan,*** *cofounder, CEO, and chief storyteller of Menlo Innovations and author of Chief Joy Officer: How Great Leaders Elevate Human Energy and Eliminate Fear*

"Robin has a joy-filled heart, and it flows like a river. She can help all of us find joy in the everyday and even during the storms of life."

—**Chuck Gaidica,** *wellness coach, speaker, author,*
and winner of multiple Emmy Awards

"Robin is a person who could make you smile even when you have nothing to smile about. She is a very joyful individual who sees positive when you only see negative, and she is able to teach you how to see it also. I am very grateful to have met such a good soul."

—**Anthony Stamatakis,** *senior business*
management consultant at Apple

"Wayne Dyer famously said when we change the way we look at things, what we look at changes. Robin lays out a practical guide to help us find joy in most every occasion. It is true that once you find joy in your heart, you find it everywhere you go. Read this book and learn how to take joy with you from this moment on."

—**Terry Bean,** *coach, keynote speaker,*
and executive producer of TEDxDetroit

"Joy . . . it's such a simple word and not always used . . . at least, not as much as it should be. Now, team that up with *messy* and you've got a new way to look at joy and have it be part of your natural conversation. *Messy Joy* by Robin Shear has given me a reason to share my joy with others and let them know that my messy joy is what makes me who I am. It's magical and relatable, and yes, I had my box of tissues right next to me as I read and reread Robin's thoughtful and inspiring words."

—**Judy Hoberman,** *president of Judy Hoberman*
and Associates, author of Selling in a Skirt:
The Secrets Women Don't Know They Know About Sales
(And What Men Should Know, Too) and Walking on the
Glass Floor: Seven Essential Qualities of Women Who Lead

"Touching. Personal. Revealing. Even funny! Robin takes you on a journey into the light even in the darkest hours."

—*Feroshia Knight, master credentialed coach, creator of Whole Person Coaching, founder of Coach Training World, and author of Become the Successful Coach You Are Meant to Be*

"Thank you for reminding us that the joy of the Lord is our strength. Yes, it meets us when we are our weakest vulnerable selves and transforms us into more than conquerors. Thank you for this work of joy."

—*Sam Thevanayagam, president and CEO of Parts Life, Inc., DeVal Lifecycle Support, and LC Engineers*

"Take *Messy Joy* to heart because the strategies in this book work! I know from firsthand experience because Robin has been my joy coach for years."

—*Zonya Foco, TV host, speaker, and author of the novel DIET FREE and Eat Real Cookbook*

"Authentic. Genuine. Vulnerable. Robin Shear's *Messy Joy* is an honest, thought-provoking, reality-filled look at how celebrating the blend of joy and messiness leads to a resilient life."

—*Warren Hébert, registered nurse, fellow of the American Academy of Nursing, and CEO of HomeCare Association of Louisiana*

"If you genuinely want to create and keep a long-term state of joy, then put this book close to your heart. Robin has shared heart-touching, real-life experiences that show how faith eliminates doubts and fears amid challenges of any size."

—*Kamal Khurana, coach and founder of Mind Tigers and author of When Mind Stops, The Magic Begins: How to Live Freely and Do What Needs to Be Done*

"Robin Shear tackles the underlying theme of what it means to live a happy, fulfilled, and purpose-driven life through her book *Messy Joy*. Shear earnestly uncovers the fact that the silver linings of life are interwoven with the realities of life, which at times can be messy. In a world of instant gratification, it's refreshing for someone to come along to remind us that we'll be okay if we just hang on for the ups and downs of life that allow us to appreciate each day."

—Dr. Celeste Bishop Stein, president and CEO of Bishop, Stein, and Associates Public Relations, Inc.

Messy
Joy

Dear Pat,

May God be with you as
you embrace and share
your own messy joys,

Robin Shear

James 1: 2-3

Messy Joy

How Joy Can Begin Before Your Difficulties End

ROBIN SHEAR

ILLUMIFY
MEDIA.COM

The views and opinions expressed in this book are those of the author and do not necessarily reflect the official policy or position of Illumify Media Global.

Any websites and URLs provided in the manuscript are active and viable as of the date of this printing but are not guaranteed to be live at any specific point in the future.

All scripture quotations, unless otherwise indicated, are taken from the Holy Bible, New International Version®, NIV®. Copyright ©1973, 1978, 1984, 2011 by Biblica, Inc.™ Used by permission of Zondervan. All rights reserved worldwide, www.zondervan.com. The "NIV" and "New International Version" are trademarks registered in the United States Patent and Trademark Office by Biblica, Inc.™

Scripture quotations marked ESV are from The Holy Bible, English Standard Version® (ESV®), copyright © 2001 by Crossway, a publishing ministry of Good News Publishers. Used by permission. All rights reserved.

Scripture quotations marked KJV from the King James Version, public domain.

Scripture quotations marked NKJV taken from the New King James Version®. Copyright © 1982 by Thomas Nelson. Used by permission. All rights reserved.

Published by
Illumify Media Global
www.IllumifyMedia.com
"Let's bring your book to life!"

Paperback ISBN: 978-1-959099-03-1

Typeset by Art Innovations (http://artinnovations.in/)
Cover design by Debbie Lewis

Printed in the United States of America

For the voiceless, who keep their hurts in.
You are not alone. You matter.
For the ones living uncontrollably imperfect lives.
You do not have to clean anything up.
For those who have loved me.
I can't see through my tears as I thank God for you.
For God, because You never stopped
fighting for me.

Consider it pure joy, my brothers and sisters, whenever you face trials of many kinds, because you know that the testing of your faith produces perseverance. Let perseverance finish its work so that you may be mature and complete, not lacking anything.
(James 1:2–4)

CONTENTS

FOREWORD

I first met Robin at the Purpose Summit 2022. When she approached me in the tunnel leading into Notre Dame Stadium, the sincerity of her care for me, a stranger at the time, was obvious. Her facial expressions communicated a depth of empathy and compassion that arrested my attention before she ever spoke a word.

In that moment, neither one of us realized that thirty days later we would reconnect to encourage each other to pursue our life callings in ways neither of us could have imagined or planned.

For those of you who have not had the opportunity to meet this Joy Coach, and may be skeptical of her title, please allow me a moment to attempt to describe her unique spirit and outlook on life.

Robin is the only adult I've ever met who eagerly awaits the end of a thunderstorm so she can take her dog for a walk and jump in every puddle she can find. Who does that?

Robin is someone who knows how to experience joy in the messy things of life. Someone whose outlook even in the midst of life's storms is always joyful, playful, adventurous, and unrestrained. Robin has the faith and mindset of a five-year-old, combined with the wisdom and experience of a centenarian.

Robin models a paradoxical blend of empathy, compassion, childlike curiosity, and joy in everything she does. Prior to meeting Robin, I used to refer to myself as a CEO—Chief Encouragement Officer. Having now experienced the "real thing," I am no longer worthy of that title.

The book you are about to read was written by a rare jewel, an angel appearing in human form.

I pray the words Robin wrote from her heart will inspire you in the same way our conversations have blessed me. Robin was a key contributor to my text to a friend that read, "This past week has been the best of my thirty-plus-year career." My friend challenged me knowing my career had been a joyride since 2003. As I searched my heart to determine if I really meant what I said, conversations and text exchanges with Robin flooded my thoughts.

Ironically, I was not Robin's client. At first, I didn't even know we were about to become lifelong friends. But I knew, beyond all doubt, that my exposure to Robin in this season was exactly what I needed in order to "choose joy" . . . especially in the messy parts of my life.

Some people spend a lifetime trying to self-promote so they can gain a platform to influence others. Based upon my experience, Robin has no interest in taking that approach to life. She prefers to stay true to her inner view and let the world experience, through their interactions with her, the joy that she cannot contain.

I encourage you to be fully present as you read these pages and participate in the exercises Robin suggests. Don't rush your way through this book. In fact, I encourage you to take a moment to jump in a few puddles in between chapters so you can experience Messy Joy for yourself.

— **Joe Colavito,**
author of *The Inside Track:*
Turnaround Principles for Business and Life,
Job Track to Joyride, and
Purpose Is More Than a Side Hustle:
It's Our Built-in GPS

ACKNOWLEDGMENTS

I love reading thank-you messages in books and on CD jackets. Maybe I am one of those warm and fuzzy connector types, but the insight into the author's life helps me feel connected to them on a personal level, and it fills my joy bucket. Well, you'll have lots of insight if you make it to the end of this book, but in case you don't, please know that I cannot take credit for this project. The Lord has blessed me with wonderful people, without whom I cannot imagine doing life, much less writing a book.

Here we go.

God: I'm going to thank You first, even if it's customary to include You last. That doesn't make sense to me. My story is Your story. Without You, Lord, there would be nothing to tell, no message to share. In the words of Isaiah 55:12, "You will go out in joy and be led forth in peace; the mountains and hills will burst into song before you, and all the trees of the field will clap their hands." Oh, that my life would clap for You, God. This beautiful, crazy life was Your idea, and the fact is, this book was Your idea too. I have no idea what You are going to do through this, but I thank You for the healing it brought me, and I pray You alone are glorified through the sharing of these stories. Meet the readers where they are, God, and love them and bring them joy as only You can. I could never thank You enough for all the ways that You love me, my family, and my friends. I acknowledge You. I thank You. I love You!

No one has a better family than I do, and I'd like to thank them one by one. They're all so important to me, I had to draw names out of an airplane barf bag on my way to a writer's retreat to decide who to thank first. *Sorry, Buddy, I'll make it up to you!*

I'd like to thank my daughter, Missy, for being so in touch with the Holy Spirit that she delivered a message from Him that made me cry . . . one that resulted in the book you are holding now. Not long ago, we were sitting in church, listening to the sermon, when she leaned over and whispered, "God is telling me that you need to write a book." I hadn't even been considering it. I was dumbfounded. I didn't want to do it. Wide-eyed, we looked into each other's souls for a second. I was scared to death because I knew it would mean facing my massive fear of rejection from a world of strangers, but the certainty in her voice and gleam in her eyes brought me tears of peace and wonder in an instant. God was speaking through my daughter.

Missy, you are practically my twin on so many levels ("Get out of my head!" . . . but don't!) and have supported me through thick and thin. Thank you, honey. Had you chosen to keep that God whisper to yourself, I doubt I would have had the courage to write this. Hearing you say those words gave me the most meaningful type of affirmation possible. If anyone is helped because of this book, it's because of your obedience when the Holy Spirit nudged you to act. You can trust Him! I so adore the way you love others with your life. You light up every room you walk into—your presence literally makes people more beautiful, because of the way their hearts and faces change when they see you. If I could go back and do it again, I'd try to live life like you. I love you!

If you haven't met my husband, Rick, you are missing out. The guy could be writing books on how to be an amazing husband and father. He even won a Father's Day contest because of it . . . ask him for the story! He goes along with my spontaneous, hair-brained ideas, works a job he's never loved just so our family can have financial stability and I can enjoy the fun, helping jobs that barely pay, and hasn't walked away during the downs that come with the ups of marriage. He has actively pursued relationships with our kids and the Lord and shines the light of what matters most to everyone around him.

Rick, thank you bringing so much goodness to our lives. Thank you for loving me enough to agree to all the insanity that comes with marrying a

*dietitian turned youth pastor turned life-coach-speaker-entrepreneur-author.
I never had to explain any of my callings to you. Nobody gets me the way you
do. All of my long hours and unfinished projects don't faze you a bit. When
I am trying to spread joy to a world that doesn't always get the concept of
spending money on it, you still encourage me to keep going. The other day
when I faced yet another business hurdle and was ready to close up shop
and apply to be a store greeter, you hugged me, calmed me down again, and
pointed out that it sounded like spiritual warfare. You were right, as is often
the case (except for whether cereal counts as dinner). I love you!*

**And thanks to the name draw, bringing up the rear is my
wonderful son, Robbie.** I remember when we found out that we were
going to have a boy, and thinking, *How will I do this? I don't know
anything about boys.* But my son changed everything. We have shared a
beautiful bond from day one, and it has allowed us to know each other
well and have a ton of fun doing it. He is a caring leader and a wonderful
man of God that I'd want to be with even if he wasn't my son. I can
confirm his classmates made the right decision when they voted him the
class clown. What a joy he has been!

*Buddy, I am so thankful for you. You bring so much fun to our family
and know just what to say to speak directly to my heart. You are the perfect
mix of crazy and thoughtful. Our conversations about faith bring so much
fulfillment to me as a mom, and I love connecting over the little things: GIFs
and TikToks, Christian rap music, and sweet cars. You were always worth
waking up early to have summer breakfasts with! I loved becoming a life
coach while you were becoming a therapist because it gave us so much to talk
about (not that we needed it . . . I remember wishing we had more time to
talk that day we drove ten hours to get lunch in Chicago). Although you've
been away at college for most of my entrepreneurial journey, you've still been
right by my side, sending me Snapchats of the clouds you know I'll want to
see, links to songs I'll want to hear, and showing up for video chats. Your
encouragement has always meant so much. I love you!*

Mom, Tracy, and Dad: (Everyone in our family is saying,
"Traaaace.") I don't even know where to start. I was the rambunctious

one, never a quiet, color-inside-the lines rule follower that was easy to be around, yet you loved me anyway. Thank you for never giving up on me. I love you endlessly, and I appreciate you more than you'll ever know. These stories and this thank-you could never do you justice. Everyone should be so loved!

My friends: In full transparency, I am surrounded by too many supportive friends to list them individually. What a "problem": there are so many—God is just that good—I could never try to name them all without missing some. If I am privileged to call you a friend, I hope you know how much I treasure you!

Health specialists I'll appreciate forever: Korah Hoffman, LMSW, MPA, and Cheryl Kennedy-Reul, PT, DPT. You have been quite the examples for others to attempt to follow. I hope you know that I try to serve my clients the way you served me. As practitioners who stop at nothing to help others, you set the bar so high!

Awesome people who particularly encouraged and supported the sharing of my message: Sandy Austin, Cindy Lambert, Marlaine Cover, Mary O'Donohue, Celeste Stein, Joe Colavito, Mike Klassen, Deb Hall, and the whole team at Illumify Media Global, Feroshia Knight, Kim Walsh Phillips and Bari Baumgartner. Thank you. This book exists, in part, because of you!

As I write these acknowledgments and reach for yet another Kleenex, the message they all point to, the thing I most want to acknowledge is this: I needed you. I needed each and every one of you. And you were THERE for me. Thank you for being by my side through the messiest of joys. I love you!

Hugs and hope,
Me

CHAPTER 1

Does Anyone Have a Perfect Life?

"I love seeing your posts on social media because they show me that life can be perfect. I want to have a perfect life too."

I didn't care if anyone judged me: I couldn't help but holler in church that day. The service had just ended, and I was collecting my things when a friend of mine approached. I hadn't seen her in a while, and she came up to hear how things were going. We chatted for a bit, and I noticed her listening intently and gazing off in the distance, wistfully. That's when she dropped the bomb.

A perfect life?

I could hardly believe my ears. I was stunned into silence. When my heartbeat returned and I could gather my thoughts, I practically shouted, "There is no such thing as a perfect life! Everyone's journey is filled with potholes!"

In that one defining moment I began to realize how my choice to share primarily about the positive was creating a false reality for my friend (and God only knew who else). Here I was, dodging the craters and banana peels of life behind the wheel with the best of them . . . all the while inadvertently setting her up to expect only smooth freeways on autopilot.

Of course, this expectation would make my friend crash right out of the gate.

The freeway reference makes me wonder
if you are also hearing Aretha Franklin sing
"Freeway of Love" in your head?
No?
How about now?

Why was I only sharing the positive with the world? I certainly had my reasons. We all have our reasons for projecting the images we choose to project. If we don't know someone's reasoning on something, we should always—always—ask, rather than assume.

This reminds me of a little game I like to play with myself:
Count all the ways I have misjudged others.

My reasons for sharing a happy life may be different than you think. I never set out to paint a picture of a blemish-free existence. In fact, I crave authenticity and find it refreshing when someone else shares a wild, uncontrollable story because it helps me feel less alone in my chaos.

The thing is, I wholeheartedly believe the structures of our families matter now and in the long run. My desire to post smiling family photos with stories of how we made memories had to do with encouraging family values and wholeness in a world that seems to treasure other things. I wanted to make a difference.

On top of that, let me throw out a question. Am I the only one who feels there is way too much complaining in the world today? We have everything—yet we go on and on about how awful life is. I mean, it just hurts my heart to know people are that unhappy. And while we're on the subject: raise your hand if you left social media due to all the negativity.

Mmm hmm, I see you, I feel you.

For these reasons, I made a personal vow to generally post fun and uplifting things to add a different voice to the noise.

The world is full of negativity, and sharing my problems wouldn't make it any better.

Or would it?

While I hoped that projecting an upbeat mindset could point other people to joy . . .

And the thought of that brought me joy, so is that selfish?

. . . it never occurred to me that I could be setting people up for unattainable goals. There is zero - absolutely *zero*—joy in contributing to that.

Enter my friend with the enormous statement in church. Here began the realization that what I shared with the world had to change if I really wanted to make a difference.

From that day forward I decided I was going to be more real. I was going to share my ups and downs, despite possibly being judged as a complainer. People were great when I started doing this, but it was hard. I was so afraid they would think I was looking for sympathy. Looking for attention.

One of the most hurtful statements I have known to be said of me is,
"She is just looking for attention."
The way I see it, if someone is truly looking for attention,
there's a reason . . .
find out why.

Even though the last thing I wanted was for someone to put me in the "needing attention" category, I did begin sharing a few more downs to go with all my ups.

At first, to dip my toe in the water, I started answering more honestly when someone asked how I was. No, they didn't get the one-act drama with all of my woes (we all know that person . . . give her a hug), but I learned to say, "I'm all right" or "Things aren't great but they'll get better," instead of "Great" or, worse yet, "Fine."

"Fine" is really girl code for an entire conversation,
probably a topic for another book.

Short, honest answers . . . toes dipped.

Then I started wading in the water. When I was having a down day, I sometimes shared a little about it on social media. Even though it was a short post along the lines of "I am just not myself today" with a song attached, it was a huge step.

Music says it best—ask Aretha.

Each time I felt the urge to share, my heart pounded out of fear, but I clicked on "Post" anyway. I don't know if anyone judged me as needy, but it usually led to some beautiful conversations. One thing is for sure: I am surrounded by wonderful people.

I was in the water, sharing without being prompted. It was progress.

And then, what I considered the cannonball of them all: I posted about my twenty-fifth attempt to resolve a long-standing joy-sucking problem in my life that I had essentially hidden from the world for two years.

For real, you'll hear about it later.

I didn't have the heart to post about the first twenty-four attempts, but number twenty-five was the prizewinner. I was feeling incredibly hopeless and posted an honest prayer, asking God to help with my mindset because it was really in the gutter. My post read, in part,

Reality check: Tomorrow I might max out and be done chasing answers to a problem. I have a procedure scheduled to remove damaged tissue . . . I cannot seem to walk away from it no matter what I try. This will be the twenty-fifth thing doctors have recommended, and I am mentally and emotionally prepared to still have pain. After two years of the cycle of getting my hopes up, doing the work, spending the money and time, and still hurting, I can't say I am approaching tomorrow with mountains of optimism. But that's okay because the healing is not up to me. I am putting this out there because it's common for people to think God is good when life is good and then wonder why He's different when life is hard. But He doesn't change!

Through it all, God, You have been GOOD. Thank You for reminding me You ARE who You say you are, whether I feel it or not. Help me to focus on facts and not feelings. And please be with my doctor's hands tomorrow. Use this entire experience for Your kingdom. I don't have to know the reasons why. Amen.

After spending fifteen minutes scrolling over two years' worth of profile posts for that thing, I hope you find it relatable. (I also hope you find a faster way to search Facebook and can teach me how it's done.)

Raw, painful prayer shared. I took the plunge.

Say what you will about posting prayers, but when I did, people offered words of comfort. They joined me in prayer. They said they could relate and felt less alone.

Whew.

I'll be honest: to get out of my own head after sharing that massive thing with the Lord and my friends on social media, I needed to go for a bike ride. I was so afraid of being judged a complainer.

Wait, God has a Facebook?

I jumped on my bike and rode along a local lakeshore as I prayed and calmed down. It helped. Before long, I felt like myself again, carefree and having fun. To celebrate, I rode full speed down the boat launch ramp, directly into the lake. Water went flying all around me, and I found myself yelling, "Because I can!" It was exactly what I needed. There must be an upside. There must! When I got home, I posted a video of it, because . . . JOY!

I felt like my prayer post was the ultimate share. Being vulnerable with my friends about hurting so badly emotionally was a monumental stretch of my comfort zone, and it seemed like the most impactful thing I could do to illustrate that a perfect life isn't the goal.

And yet, here we are: you (have we met?), me, and maybe even someone else reading this book besides my mom.

Hi, Mom!
Thank you for being my most loyal fan.
I am sorry for all the spilled milk.

This thing you are holding is a book filled with much, much bigger shares, and I am the author.

Splish splash, I am taking a bath.

Yup, I don't even know you, and I am handing you *the cannonball*.

For heaven's sake, why??

Two reasons.

One: I am a joy coach. Yup, that's a thing. I am on a serious mission to help people choose joy when the circumstances say it's impossible, because it's a choice that makes all the difference.

I care so much about spreading this message that I have really, really started sharing.

Never in my wildest dreams did I think I would create a YouTube channel to share stories with strangers around the world about what it's like to seek joy despite the difficulties of life or—you have got to be kidding me—write a book on the subject.

Again, here we are. Hello. Hi!

Holy cow, this is scary.

Even though I am shaking in my boots, I am about to tell you things I haven't told anyone outside of family, a couple of extremely safe friends, and paid professionals.

Why?

Because of reason number two.

Two: God Himself told me to.

If that's not your thing, let's love each other anyway.
And maybe you can keep reading.

While sharing big was never my plan and writing a book was never on my list, I have to trust that it's the right thing to do.

Evidently God thinks there is good in it, because He made it clear I need to do this and He is always, always good.

Who am I to misjudge Him?

Messy Joy Spill-Your-Guts Journal Questions:

1. If you are being 100 percent honest, what are your beliefs about having a perfect life?

2. When you are hurting, do you let people in? Why or why not?

3. Whom do you feel safe sharing with? What do you appreciate about this person that you would like to model for others?

4. What song/s have you felt contained parts of your story?

5. Are you quick to judge others? How accurate have your assumptions been?

6. Are you afraid of being judged by others? Where does this fear come from? How is it serving or harming you? How does it connect to the amount of joy in your life?

7. If a friend made a statement about your life based on what you share (on social media or otherwise), what might it be? How do you feel about this?

8. Do you know anyone who gets put into the "looking for attention" category? Why might that be, and how might you be able to truly help this person?

9. When you are not "fine," what are some more honest answers you might feel comfortable giving? How does an honest answer affect people's ability to love you? What effect might that have on the joy in your life? How might it affect the joy level of the people you are giving more honest answers to?

10. If you share your heart on social media (or elsewhere), who would be most likely to respond with an encouraging word? How do their responses make you feel?

11. What helps you feel like "you" when you need to get out of your own head? When's the last time you participated in this action, activity, or experience? Would you go so far as to say that it brings you joy?

12. Do you believe that God talks to you? If yes, has God talked to you in the past? When and how? If you don't believe God talks to you, what are your beliefs about God?

CHAPTER 2

Joy and Happiness— Aren't They the Same Thing? Who Cares?

O ur daughter, Missy, picked out her wedding dress yesterday morning. The joy of the moment is still carrying me today. I'm feeling a little floaty. It felt like we lived a dream.

A full twenty-four hours later, my heart is swelling at the memory of the look on her face. This might be a mom thing, but just imagining what she looked like is enough to fill my eyes with tears as I type. My tears of joy were spraying all over that shop yesterday.

It's a good thing I was packing (Kleenex, that is).

Missy tried on about fifteen dresses, and they were all gorgeous. It was hard to narrow them down. It was so much fun seeing the admiration on the faces of the sales attendants and other ladies as she came out of the fitting room. The dreamy way she looked in one dress after another made me just shake my head in wonder, tears flinging all over the pink velvet mom couch.

I remember saying, "You need to look less amazing, or we are never going to be able to choose!"

But when she came out of the dressing room in that beautiful gown, in the one that was made for her, the look on her face said it all . . . her joy made her eyes sparkle in a way that words can't describe: it was the one.

Joy.

Yes, joy was alive and well in that bridal shop.

You're here to dig into joy. You want to feel more of it because:

- Your life's pretty great. Mountaintop moments (like the one I had yesterday) aren't uncommon. You know that joy feels amazing, and you'd like to soak up more so you can keep giving it away.
- Your life is messy. Real talk, it might even be a bit of a train wreck sometimes. Things aren't in order, and they're not going to be. You wonder if you can have joy now, before life is cleaned up. You'd like to be able to share joy with other people someday, but in the spirit of keeping it real, right now you admit you need some joy just to get through the day.
- You're somewhere in the middle, living out a pretty great mess, riding the highs and lows of life. You're not complaining, but you are seeking more joy to benefit from personally and to have some left over to share with the world around you.

Do you, like my friend in the previous chapter, believe a perfect life is possible? When you read that story, did you think, *I don't get it, what's wrong with wanting a perfect life?* or *She's crazy, she'll never have a perfect life!* or something in the middle like, *A perfect life sounds impossible, but maybe if I try hard enough . . .*

And then we have a select few who are still wondering,
"Yeah, but did they kick you out of church for shouting?"

Be honest. What's your gut saying right now?

And the big question, the real reason you're here: do you believe a perfect, social-media-worthy, cleaned-up life is necessary before true joy can enter in?

Do you believe you can have messy joy?

I am here to tell you—thanks be to God!—even the messiest lives can still have joy scrambled in.

Perfect lives are a myth. We do not have to wait until everything is just right to experience joy. Heck, we don't even have to land all our Kleenexes into the trash can first. We can have joy and we can have it now.

How do I know? Put me in, coach! Pick me! I know because I am living a messy, joy-filled life.

If we've had the privilege of meeting, you'll probably say I am a joyful person. Now that I'm known as a joy coach, people often call me "Joy," forgetting my actual name.

I love it. It totally beats "Pain."

After interacting, people have often said, "You exude joy."

I am a definition person. I hope they are talking about the type of exuding that means displaying a quality openly and not the "discharging a smell slowly and steadily" type.

I've got plenty of joy to share, but my life is messy. Very messy. If you don't believe me, keep reading. I am about to tell you things I have kept hidden for years. If you need proof that you can have messy joy, I hope that my stories will be all the proof you need, no matter how hard they are for me to share.

*I'll be honest, I am feeling so much resistance as I type this that
I have a different kind of tears in my eyes now. Sharing the stuff
that isn't upbeat isn't easy at all. But you are worth it.
And healing would be good for me too.*

I know a bunch of people who have messy joy in their lives. They have been my joy coaching clients. They live in all corners of the world and are different as night and day, but they have this in common: they are seeking and finding joy despite their circumstances. They are authors, parents, athletes, psychologists, students, educators, skilled tradesmen, doctors, entrepreneurs.

They are real people experiencing everyday struggles, and for confidentiality reasons, I can't elaborate on their stories, but they are facing diagnoses, medical disabilities, rejection, failure, broken relationships, self-doubt, financial strain, depression, uncertainty, burnout, difficult decisions, grief.

Not one of them has a perfect life. In fact, I got the term *train wreck* from the way some of them have described their lives.

But they now experience joy among the wreckage. It's messy, but it's joy nonetheless.

You see, messy joy isn't about perfection. It's about possibility. It's possible for us and it's possible for you.

But what is joy exactly?

It seems funny to ask about what joy is. Of course we know what it is. Right?

Every time I speak to an audience, I ask that question. And every time, the answers are different. Every single time.

Gosh, maybe we don't know joy as well as we thought.

Why is that? Why isn't there an obvious definition we all agree on? Because we rarely stop the crazy train of life long enough to think about it. Honestly, when's the last time you thought about it? Have you ever really gone there?

If you were to ask yourself right now how to define joy and happiness, what would you say?

How do they actually feel in your body? Where do you feel them?

And it doesn't help that joy is kind of . . . fluffy. It isn't like pizza, something that's clearly visible and easy to define. It's out there a bit, it's more subjective, more dependent on our personal views. We know it when we feel it, but describing it is a bit more challenging.

Like an unstoppable end-of-winter dry-skin itch.

The important thing is for you to know how you personally define joy so you know what you are going after . . . so you'll be able to know with certainty when you've obtained it. It needs to be a clear destination. When you put "joy" into the GPS of your life, what exactly are you aiming for?

And, to add another layer, are you going after joy, or are you heading for happiness?

Does it matter?

Yes.

The truth is, while happiness and joy have some similarities, they are not the same, and knowing the difference will be foundational to appreciating what's actually present in your own life.

When you stop and think about it, it's interesting how interchangeable joy and happiness are in our culture. If you search online for quotes or songs about joy, lists featuring happiness will populate.

A quote that I love: "Focus on the good and joy will follow."
A song you have to check out: "Joy" by for King & Country.

But are they really interchangeable? It's time to settle this. Let's turn to the source of all wisdom and knowledge: Google.

Google's definition of happiness: "The state of being happy."

Wait. Come on! Is that the best you can do?

Similar words: contentment, pleasure, satisfaction, cheerfulness, merriment, gaiety, joy, jollity (*that's a new one*), glee.

Google's definition of happy: "Feeling or showing pleasure or contentment."

Similar words: contented, cheerful, merry, joyful, jovial, jolly, joking, jocular *(look it up, I have no idea)*, gleeful, carefree, untroubled, delighted, smiling.

Google's definition of joy: "A feeling of great pleasure or happiness."

Seriously? Who writes this stuff?

Similar words: delight, jubilation, triumph, exultation, happiness, glee, exhilaration, ebullience, exuberance, elation, euphoria, bliss.

Bliss reminds me of when my grandma would say something dingy and my grandpa would declare, "They say ignorance is bliss. Well, your grandma is full of bliss." Let's hope he was being jocular.

Wow, I'm not super impressed with these definitions. In fact, this may seem stupid because I'm only two chapters in, and I'm not a very big fish, but I am taking on Google. I don't completely agree with the Google definitions of happiness and joy.

It was nice knowing you. Here begins my epitaph.

Basically, Google is saying that happiness is being filled with contentment, and joy is a state of extra happiness. Essentially happy and happy 2.0.

There has to be more. Let's see what the leading scientific and professional psychology organization in the United States says.

The American Psychological Association's definition of happiness: "An emotion of joy, gladness, satisfaction, and well-being."

The American Psychological Association's definition of joy: "A feeling of extreme gladness, delight, or exultation of the spirit arising from a sense of well-being or satisfaction."

I love and respect me some psychologists, but here we are again with happy and happy 2.0.

I am going to put this in writing: I do not have a psychology degree. I do not claim to have one. There are so many people with advanced psychology degrees who are smarter than I am. But I know joy down to my core, and my definition is different. How do I know joy? I have seen it in all of my callings:

- While it hasn't been perfect, joy has been very present in my family life. It made me absolutely love all of my kids' ages, especially the teen years. We had a blast then, and we're having one now too.

- As a dietitian working with people with scary diagnoses and even scarier backstories (trauma can lead to eating disorders, and people with them made up the bulk of my nutrition counseling practice), my work wasn't just about the food; it was about quality of life. It was about joy.

- Later, serving in youth ministry with hundreds of kids who were filled with angst, pressure, and confusion, I saw how joy was like oxygen in even the most suffocating situations.

- And finally, serving as an activity director and life enrichment team member at four facilities where senior citizens lived, many of whom had Alzheimer's and other forms of dementia, I saw firsthand the difference joy made. We went on mystery trips, learned seated kickboxing routines, told stories, and laughed until our sides hurt. Joy impacts this often-forgotten population very, very directly.

Quick joy tip: Do you want to visit with seniors and share joy?
Our facilities and schedules were jammed at the holidays with kindhearted
choirs, school groups, and visitors, almost to the point of exhaustion.
Want good news? The seniors love singing, conversation,
and activity all year round. Yay!

The thing I want you to have? It's better than happy 2.0. It's deeper. It's richer.

My understanding of joy is rooted in the Bible.

Wow, first she takes on Google and now she drops the B word.
What will happen in the next chapter?

Now, I know—and cherish!—the fact that we are all from different backgrounds. Our differences make us interesting. I love meeting people who are different. In fact, friends have said that my superpower is connecting with people who are different than I am.

Even though I was hoping my superpower
would be flying or invisibility.
Or even a functioning sense of direction.

The truth is, as much as I love our differences, I would much rather dig into how we are alike. So I recognize that sharing my faith background in the beginning of a book can be risky. I don't want you to chuck this book in a donation bin before you even finish it.

But I cannot tell my story without including my roots which is my Christian faith. I can't separate myself from my foundation, and I wouldn't want to. My relationship with Jesus is everything to me. However, I realize you may be coming from a very different place. Can we just agree not to judge each other? I've got friends who are Muslim, Jewish, Christian, Hindu, atheist, agnostic, and everything in between.

No Pastafarians yet, but maybe someday.

Even though biblical references will be woven throughout this book, they aren't intended to alienate anyone. I'm going to love you and encourage you to keep reading even if you have different beliefs. Is this so I can shove my faith down your throat? No, it's so I can share the depth of my understanding of joy with you. Whether or not we share the same religious beliefs, I believe that reading this book might help you to know more joy than you ever thought possible.

Whew! I'm exhaling. I needed you to know my heart. It's so important to me that in sharing my beliefs, I don't make you feel singled out. We are on the same team, the human team. Go us!

So, what's the biblical definition of joy? The back of my *NIV Life Application Study Bible* (the one I'll reference throughout this book unless otherwise noted) has a dictionary. I love that thing and use it all the time to look up words people tend to take for granted.

Bible dictionary definition of happiness:

"A state of well-being and contentment."

Bible dictionary definition of joy:

"Emotion evoked by well-being, success or good fortune; gladness or delight."

Wait, what? All that, and happy and happy 2.0 are in my Bible's dictionary? Shoot.

I'll admit, I was hoping they would be more distinct. But even I am not stupid enough to argue with the Bible. So, as we look at a few of the Bible verses that include joy (the word *joy* appears nearly two hundred times in the Bible), we'll see if God's actual word (and not the dictionary) will help us have a better understanding of what joy is and why it matters so much.

Until then, if you're still with me, let me share with you my personal definitions of happiness and joy.

Hey, good lookin'! So glad you're here!

Maybe these "Robinized" definitions will help you know what to put in your GPS.

Robin's definition of happiness:

Happiness is the brief positive feeling that results when a situation is in your favor. Happiness is always dependent on circumstances. It usually subsides when the circumstances change. It tends to be a personal experience and often ties into our culture's "It's all about me" thinking.

For example, what's your favorite food? Potato chips? Donuts?

Shout-out to the person who said, "Brussels sprouts."
There's a special spot for you in heaven.

If you, like my sister, Tracy, said chocolate and you break off a piece of Ghirardelli and let it slowly melt in your mouth, your taste buds will shout, "Happy!" It's amazing. (However, Tracy prefers to inhale her chocolate.) But it's your experience, so no one else will feel what you are feeling unless they are also eating their favorite food. And when the chocolate is gone, your emotions return to normal. The happiness subsides because it's a fleeting emotion. There's nothing wrong with it, but by nature, it comes and goes with the circumstances. That's why chasing happiness can be fun but also a bit like a roller coaster ride. If it's the only thing we seek, we will find ourselves continually disappointed and exhausted.

Next up, let's look at joy.

Robin's definition of joy:

Joy is a longer-lasting inner effervescence for life itself. It's more of a way of being, a positive way of viewing things, than a reaction to stimuli, though it can sometimes be triggered by circumstances. It feels great, like happiness, but on a longer-term basis. It's deeper and richer than happiness. Joy is contagious. It feels so good, we want other people to experience it, and we share it without even trying. There are times when we feel joy naturally and other times when we must choose joy. It's a fruit of the Spirit, so it's a gift from God that is given when we remain close to Him.

> **"The fruit of the Spirit is love, joy, peace, patience, kindness, goodness, faithfulness, gentleness, self-control."**
> *(Galatians 5:22 NASB)*

This is why I know I felt joy when I saw Missy standing there in her wedding dress. I wasn't even wearing it. But her joy in finding the dress of her dreams to marry the man of her dreams was so contagious, I couldn't help but be swept up by it. More than twenty-four hours later, I still feel it. Will I feel it forever? No, that's not the promise of joy. Joy is lasting, but it's not permanent. Outside of eternal life in Jesus, I don't believe it's realistic that we can obtain something positive that will last forever. But that's not the goal of joy, or of this book.

The goal of joy is resilience. Resilience is what you experience when the storms of life—the messes—don't knock you down for good. Resilience helps you rise again. This quality, among many others, is what makes joy a worthwhile investment.

You might be surprised to know that just a few hours after Missy got her wedding dress, someone tried to rob her of $750. It was crazy. We needed to choose joy just for the sake of the resilience it brought. It's a wild story called "How to Dig for Joy in the Rubble of Your Life," and you can read what happened on my Joy Bites blog at joytotheworldcoaching.com. If you want to chat more often, subscribe while you're there.

If the goal of joy is resilience, the goal of *Messy Joy* is to help you learn how to experience more resilience in your imperfect life by cultivating joy. Let's focus more of our time and attention on the things that have lasting impact. Let's recognize that happiness is okay and fun to enjoy in the moment, but choosing also to nurture joy can bring fulfillment in the long run.

Throughout *Messy Joy*, we'll look at where joy comes from. It's going to be different for each of us, which is awesome. To make sure your time here is well spent, you'll be able to apply the concepts in the chapters to your own life by answering journal questions. Let me urge you to slow down and take time to do this, even if you've never journaled before. Just grab a pad of paper or your phone and answer the questions honestly.

Secondly, let me encourage you to start filling out the Joy Bucket List inside the back cover. This is a place where you can be reminded of the things that make you feel most alive. You won't be able to fill it out in one sitting. The more you think about joy, the more it will bubble up and become clear to you. We'll come back to this list often. Be sure to expand your Joy Bucket List as thoughts about joy come to you. Later, I'll share a story of a time when I was thankful to have created my list before I really needed it. Do not neglect this important (and fun) step. Trust me and get started now.

Fun fact: you'll soon learn that the reason it's called a Joy Bucket is because once you get going on acknowledging the joy in your life, a cup will never do.

"You prepare a table before me in the presence of my enemies.
You anoint my head with oil; my cup overflows."
(Psalm 23:5)

A cup? Of course it overflows.
I am in no position to correct the Bible.
But let's give them grace. They probably didn't have five-gallon buckets back
then. Get yourself a joy bucket.

Messy Joy is essentially a workbook. Do the work. Take the time. You are worth it. Let's make sure that you're not staying on the surface, just skimming the stories, questioning the sanity in my inner dialogue and rethinking old song lyrics. Let's make sure that you really are learning how to find messy joy.

Messy Joy Spill-Your-Guts Journal Questions:

1. Is your life pretty great, messy, or a combination (a pretty great mess)? How do you know?
2. What are your thoughts about having enough joy in your life to be able to give some away?
3. Do you believe a perfect life is possible? Share your thoughts here.
4. Do you believe a perfect, social-media-worthy, cleaned-up life is necessary before joy can enter in? Do you believe you can have messy joy?
5. What quality do people say you exude? How do you feel about this?
6. What is your personal definition of joy? Dig deep.
7. In your own words, how do you define happiness?
8. What thoughts do you have about the difference between joy and happiness?
9. How do happiness and joy actually feel in your body when they show up? Where do you feel them? What sensations do you experience? Get as specific as possible.
10. What do you spend the majority of your time seeking: happiness or joy? Why do you think this is?
11. Do you have any favorite quotes or songs that help you focus on joy?
12. What thoughts do you have about my sharing of my faith and using it as the basis for my understanding of joy?

13. If your faith background is different than mine, why are you planning to proceed with (or end) your reading of this book? Are there any helpful takeaways here?

14. Are you drawn to people who are different than you are, similar to you, or a mixture? What might this say about you?

15. My Christian faith is my foundation. What's your foundation?

16. Share your thoughts about my definition of happiness. Do you agree or disagree with it? Does this affect your definition of happiness?

17. Looking at my definition of joy, what thoughts come up for you? How does this influence your definition of joy, if at all?

18. As you begin to think about the things that bring joy to you, what are the first few things that make your list? Be sure to add them to your Joy Bucket List inside the back cover. Refer back to this list often!

CHAPTER 3

Where Was God When I Got Hurt?

This is the beginning of a story that falls in the "life's not perfect for anyone and here's proof" category.

A very dear friend of mine signs his text messages to me with GIG. Then he knows I'm going to sign mine with ATT. He doesn't work gigs, and I don't work in communications.

But we believe that God is good. All the time. GIG. ATT.

Dan the Man, you're so awesome, I wrote about you in my book!

Hang out with any group of Christians for long and chances are, someone will say this. Sometimes they'll say it so often you'll want to hit the mute button. They'll say "God is good" when they feel blessed. When something favorable happens. When they feel His love.

"God is good," the first will say. "All the time," the next replies.

And it's true. But have you ever heard anyone say it after a tragedy? When an ambulance passes with its lights flashing and sirens blaring? (God is good.) When the news is filled with horrific stories of the latest school shooting? (All the time.) Have you spoken it in your darkest moments? Do you believe God is good even then? Let that settle for a minute.

Is praising God on your Joy Bucket List?
Would it change the amount of joy in your life?

When things are hard, when life is messy, we don't often praise God for His goodness. We don't thank Him for His presence. Instead we ask, *Where in the heck are You, God?*

Where was God when I got hurt?

First, let me tell you what happened.

It's crazy looking back at that day, to think how one split-second decision impacted so much afterward. It seemed like one minute, I was posting a smiling family photo from the driveway, and the next, I was in the ER.

To anyone who is nodding their head in understanding, remembering their
own life-changing split-second decision
that made life messy in a hurry, I get you.
You are not alone.

We were on our second annual 6-Pack Ski Trip, which was a Christmas gift from my husband, Rick, and me to our two kids and their sweethearts: The 6-Pack. We rented a condo four hours north and could not wait to enjoy two full days of skiing together.

While we love to make memories as a group, the reality is, we tend to split up on ski trips, because we are all at various skill levels. Rick is the most experienced skier and loves to rip down challenging black diamond runs. Our son, Robbie, loves hitting black diamonds and blue mountains on his snowboard. Missy, Nick (Missy's now-husband), and Mary (Robbie's now-wife) enjoy skiing down the fast blue mountain trails. Me? I just hope to stay mostly upright on the green hills and connect with new skiers who are the same age on the outside as I am on the inside.

We decided day one would be a night ski and, after enjoying great conversation, food, and laughter in the condo, headed over to ski for four hours. As this was only my third time skiing ever, I was good with a short first night. To get a sense of how much skiing stretches my comfort zone (proving how desperate I am for family time), you can read about our crazy first-ever 6-Pack ski trip in a blog I posted called "Get Out of Your Comfort Zone: Get on the Chairlift" (search for the story on joytotheworldcoaching.com under the "Joy Bites Blog" tab.)

So the thing is, skiing was weird for me from the start of this trip. I'm not talking new-skier weird; I'm talking physically and mentally weird. Every run I made that night, I felt slow and weak. I am "small but mighty" (girl code for "short") and generally feel pretty strong. That night, I felt like 50 percent of my strength was missing.

As I picked up speed going downhill, I found myself praying I'd be strong enough to stop the right way. No one wants to stop the wrong way: nailing innocent victims, sending them flying like human bowling pins.

But another weird thing was happening . . . I couldn't think fast enough. It was like there was a one-second mental lag. Being off by a second when you're typing is one thing, but skiing when you're mentally off is just plain risky. It felt like my brain cells and muscle cells were dredged in thick molasses . . . everything moved more slowly.

We had just recovered from COVID-19 at Christmastime (if you want to hear our COVID story, read "When Your Family Has COVID-19 and You Are Grateful for God's Goodness" at joytotheworldcoaching.com, under the "Joy Bites Blog" tab). Although my case was never confirmed with a test, doctors said I was presumed to have COVID. The only thing I can chalk my weirdness on the slopes up to is possible aftereffects of the virus.

We went back to the condo for a mountain of food, games, and connection. I slept well and faced day two with optimism. However, the very first run on a larger green hill found me nearly out of control. The molasses feeling still plagued my brain and legs.

My fear for the well-being of other skiers told me I needed to return to a smaller hill immediately. I was sad to part ways with my family so early in the day because we had planned to stay together for a little while. Being together is such a huge source of joy for us.

Is time with your family on your Joy Bucket List? Hint!

We agreed to meet up at lunch, and I skied off to the chairlift alone. As I rode up over the resort's smallest hill, I admired people going over the jumps along the edge. It was interesting to watch which part of the jump they aimed for and how they landed. As I watched, a spontaneous idea began brewing.

Here's a bonus Joy Bucket List hint:
does spontaneity belong on your list?
If yes, you are one of my people!
If no, I love you anyway.
I'll just do it in a more scheduled way.

I thought, *Dang, it would be so much fun to practice on this hill while my family is gone and get really strong. And then it would be really fun to start mastering these jumps so I can surprise them at lunch!*

I know, right?

You know the scene in *Titanic* where Rose jumps out of the lifeboat to stay with Jack on the sinking ship (young love!) and he says, "Rose, you're so stupid! Why'd you do that, huh? You're so stupid, Rose!"?

This is the part where you can call me Rose.

I really thought it was a good idea to try to get strong and surprise my family with the jumps.

I would like to say my stupidity ended there. But when I got off the chairlift, I heard familiar voices. Turning around in disbelief, I saw the faces of my five family members. They'd given up their awesome black and blue hills to be with me on the tiniest of greens. Time together was more important than adventure (which for all of us is another big source of joy).

Adventure: check your Joy Bucket List!

I was in tears. I felt so loved. They excitedly told me they wanted to go down the jumps while I simultaneously went down the easy hill; this way we could still be together. Wow!

In a rush of emotion and connection, all I wanted was to be with them. And that's when I announced my stupid decision to join them on the jumps when I wasn't ready.

Yup.

There were a bunch of jumps in a row. I studied how the first four 6-Pack members sailed over them with ease. With no problem, Rick, Robbie, Nick, and Mary all made it to the bottom.

It was my turn. My heart was pounding as I took off. I found myself flying fast—too fast—toward the first jump. I realized too late there was no way my sludgy muscles could slow me down in time to approach the first jump under control. As I neared it, I knew I was in trouble. But I went for it, because, Rose.

What happened next was a blur. All I remember was flailing, feeling like I was twenty feet high (it was probably only ten) and thinking, *Oh no!* before landing hard on the back of my head. I smacked so hard (oh, the sound!) that the inertia flung me forward and I finally landed facedown, unable to move, in shock. It was wild.

I didn't move.

I felt like I was on a world globe model that some mischievous elementary school kid was spinning at full force. I seriously thought I was going to fling off. Sitting up was out of the question, it made me so dizzy and nauseated. For a brief time I was trapped between jumps one and two before Missy came tearing down after me to see if I was okay.

She could not see me from the top, and the others couldn't see me from the bottom.

Missy quickly realized I was not well and somehow helped me scoot out of the path so other skiers didn't nail me. I don't remember it. Before she could ski down to get Rick, he was coming up on the chairlift. We relieved her so she didn't have to see me like that. I implored her to go and have fun with the others and send pictures. The last thing I wanted was to ruin their day. It was their gift!

Bundled up in thick layers and suddenly hotter than heck, with sweat pouring down my body and my purple helmet still strapped on, I was thankful for the snow. I lay facedown in that beautiful, ice-cold stuff for a good twenty to thirty minutes, refusing to ask for help. (Can you relate? We'll dig into the whole "asking for help" thing in chapter 4). But in those moments, I was convinced I would eventually be able to walk to the top of the mountain or ski down to the chairlift. I did not want to make a scene and be rescued by the ski patrol's snowmobile sled thing with its sirens and lights.

I tried to sit upright so I could then try to stand. And that's when the vomiting started.

Again and again, I tried to get up, got sick, and covered it with fresh snow, hoping no one would see. I wanted to leave that mountain on my own terms so badly. It was awful to continue the cycle, feeling helpless and determined at the same time. Rick kept telling me I needed help, and finally I gave in and let him get the ski patrol. The snowmobile sled thing pulled up, lights flashing. They loaded me into the sled. We took off, and I didn't look at anyone so they couldn't look directly at me either.

This is exactly how Robbie used to play
hide and seek when he was really little.
He hid with his eyes closed tight,
hands covering them, so no one could see him.

Getting lost in the wonder of childlike thinking—
should it be on your Joy Bucket List?

Once the ski patrol team got me inside the first aid area for a systems check, they quickly determined I needed to be seen at the hospital. It was unbelievable to me. It was just a bump. People hit their heads all the time. But they helped me, dizzy as all get out, climb into our car, and Rick drove me to town.

Because hospitals allowed limited visitors due to COVID, my poor husband had to wait in the car, hoping I could answer the admission questions correctly; he wasn't able to return to skiing. I felt terrible about it. He'd waited a year for this trip and spent it in a hospital parking lot.

They whisked me back to triage and did all of the usual concussion tests, including an MRI, which was fine. I felt awful physically and mentally, but at least there was no brain bleed.

Something led the team to believe I had broken my neck, and they put one of those massive hard collars around it. It should have been scary. But I was so glad to have help getting better, I focused on what I was grateful for instead, and I felt peaceful.

Gratitude is a powerful source of joy. Is it on your Joy Bucket List?

I was so grateful for the presence of God. I never had to ask, *Where in the heck are You?* because I could feel Him and see Him at work everywhere. I should have been afraid. But He was so obviously at work for my good, everywhere I looked, I found peace and joy.

"Have I not commanded you? Be strong and courageous.
Do not be afraid; do not be discouraged, for the LORD your God
will be with you wherever you go."
(Joshua 1:9)

God sent the snow that felt so good on my face.

He was right there, saving me from being hit by other skiers.

God somehow made it possible for the puking to stop when I got moved to the snow ambulance.

He got me off the mountain.

He gave me family to share love with.

He gave me access to health care and then made the medical team smart enough to figure out how to care for me.

He sent help to peel off complicated layers of ski clothing when I wasn't even sure if I could pull my arms through the sleeve holes.

He provided warmth through the hospital's heated blankets when my temperature started to go haywire from lying facedown in the snow for so long. At one point I needed five heated blankets.

God kept my entire family safe, and He even let the kids have fun and make memories together.

He made it possible for photos and messages to arrive on my phone just when I needed them, and He gave me strength to bring the phone up to my eyes when I thought I was too weak.

God was with me when I had my accident. He was before me, behind me, above me, and around me. He was good again and again.

It was funny: my body felt like absolute crap in the ER, but my experience was filled with joy. I swear, I'm not on any meds as I type. I had never felt worse physically, but I had tears of gratitude running down my cheeks the whole time. It didn't matter that I was too weak to wipe them. They kept falling, and I kept telling the Lord, *Thank You*, and He kept giving me reasons to be joyful.

Here's one example. I found out that my nurse and I have the same birthday. This might not be a big deal to you, but you need to know that in our house, we love birthdays! Plus, connection is a very rich source of joy for me, and I couldn't wait to learn how my nurse planned to celebrate his birthday, wondering if we'd do anything in common.

Is connection on your Joy Bucket List? Let's grow that thing!

My nurse shared that he had a different view of birthdays, that they were no big deal. I wasn't having it. I made it real clear right then and there that I was thankful he was born and appreciated so much how he was there with his skills and knowledge in the exact moment when I needed care. The exact moment! To me it was a very big deal that he was born. I encouraged him to celebrate the fact that he made a difference and mattered to someone.

He planned to celebrate differently that year, and I was back to being thankful. More tears of joy.

After spending a long chunk of the day lying there alone, waiting on tests, pouring encouragement into the medical staff who occasionally checked in, and praying my heart out while I enjoyed the thought of the fun my sweet family was having, I got good news. Thanks be to God, I did not break my neck, and I could be released. I could go back to the ski lodge and see my family! I was diagnosed with a concussion (shocker) and told to take it easy for seven to ten days. They told me I should be fine in about a week if I didn't hit my head again.

God is so cool, because not only did He protect my neck and prevent all kinds of devastation despite my stupidity, but somehow He strengthened me enough to be able to walk out of that hospital on my own. I could not believe it. Honestly, I'd call this level of healing miraculous. It makes no sense to me that navigating the hospital hallways was mentally possible, let alone walking unassisted after my difficulty sitting upright earlier.

Isn't all healing miraculous? How does it happen down at the nuclear level, for our good? Have you ever really thought about it? Focusing on the miracle of healing was such a joy bringer, I felt like skipping. No worries, I settled for walking unsteadily.

Check your list! Does it bring you joy to dwell on miracles?

There were even more God sightings as the events of that monumental day came to a close:

- God allowed me to have a husband who was willing to give up a whole day of his favorite kind of fun to wait, alone, in a hospital parking lot for me with no communication from the hospital.

- He gave me kids that rushed to the lodge for massive, loving embraces when we returned.

- He gave Robbie the ability to admit his sadness at feeling he was at fault for my going over the jump, something he had carried in his heart all day as he worried about me in the ER. I had no idea. My heart hurt more for him than my head did.

- And God allowed me to tell Robbie that the jumps had been part of my plan all along and that I was responsible for my own choices, relieving him of any guilt.

- He also gave me reason to celebrate. Ever since learning to ski, because it is such a big stretch of my comfort zone, I have celebrated by buying a ski resort sticker for each place we experience. Even though the memories of the trip were different than I had anticipated, God was with me, and He was with my family, and He did let us have meaningful experiences there. Oh, you can bet I got that sticker before we left. I proudly put it on my helmet, celebrating the good things God did, dang it! If you want to see the actual moment when it all came together, watch "One Take on Joy: The Mess Becomes the Message" on YouTube. (Fun fact: If you read an excerpt from this book before it was published, and saw my goofy photo with the purple ski helmet on, you'll recognize that still image because it was taken from this video.)

So yes, my friend, life is going to throw each of us a curveball. Or fifty. Things will go differently than we hope or plan. I wasn't planning to wind up with a concussion; I was hoping to have fun with my family.

In truth, there will be much greater difficulties than what I experienced. Perhaps you are reading this in a much more dire situation, thinking, *I wish all I had was a concussion.* I want you to know my heart hurts for you. It truly does. But the more important thing is that you know the Lord Himself hurts for you. Need proof?

"Jesus wept."
(John 11:35)

This . . . this is the God we serve. The God who has the same feelings we have. He wants for us to have fullness of life and to live according to His plan, one that includes doing life very much in connection with Him.

"I have come that they may have life,
and that they may have it more abundantly."
(John 10:10 NKJV)

If you think connection brings joy to you, imagine what it brings to the one who designed and made you for it.

No matter what you are facing, no matter how messy your life currently is, when you are tempted to ask God, *Where in the heck are You?* I instead urge you to open your heart, open your eyes, and look for Him. Where is He? You won't have to look hard.

You will see that He is all around you, going before and behind you . . . being good.

Because God is good.

All the time.

Messy Joy Spill-Your-Guts Journal Questions:

1. Do you honestly believe God is good all the time? When you hear this expression, what thoughts do you have?

2. Can you think of a time you praised God for His goodness during a tragedy? A difficulty? If you are experiencing one now, how might praising Him bring you joy? (And is praising God on your Joy Bucket List?)

3. Look up the definition of the word *praise*. Does this change anything for you as you consider praising God during hard times?

4. Write about a time you anticipated one outcome and experienced something totally different. What happened and what did you learn?

5. Looking back on the toughest time in your life, what can you be thankful for?

6. Does time with certain people, maybe your family, bring joy? Why do you think this might be? How can you express this to them this week? Are they on your Joy Bucket List?

7. Think of a time you wish you could go back to and do differently, to prevent difficulties. What lessons can you carry forward?

8. Is spontaneity on your Joy Bucket List? Explain.

9. What does your sense of adventure say about you?

10. There are times in life when we need to jump and other times when we need to pass. In certain moments, how have you gone

about making decisions that turned out to be for your good in the end?

11. Think back on one of the scariest experiences in your life. Allow yourself to feel the pain, knowing the intensity won't last. Take all the time you need to answer this question honestly: where was God?

12. Is gratitude a source of joy for you? How frequently do you choose to dwell on it? Are you as quick to show gratitude to others as you'd like to be? Name one practical way this can be improved.

13. List fifty things you are grateful for. Don't let the number intimidate you. Just let go and feel true gratitude. Get down to the nitty gritty. Think small. What happens to your joy as you focus on gratitude?

14. Connection can be a powerful source of joy. Whom do you feel most connected to and why? Do they know?

15. Write about times you have felt a true connection with a stranger. What did it do to your joy? What does this say about joy?

16. Do you like to dwell, or meditate, on miracles? What effect does it have on your joy? Are you aware of any miracles happening right now?

17. Write about a time you intentionally celebrated the things God was doing in your life.

18. How can you personally train yourself to shift your mindset from *God, where in the heck are you?* to *God, You are with me in the hurt, and You are good?*

CHAPTER 4

Why Is It So Hard to Ask for Help?

Have you ever wanted to make snow angels in a bikini or pull out your toenails with tweezers?

I would rather do those things than ask for help.

Can you relate?

Actually the snow angel thing is pretty fun; I need to do that again. It must be the connection between spontaneity and joy . . . for me. Not so much for my family. They usually resort to bathing suit snow angels only after I resort to the "but what if I die tomorrow?" speech.

Sorry, not sorry, guys.

Personally, I dread the thought of putting people in a position where they feel obligated to do something for me. Just the fear of being one more thing on someone's to-do list makes me want to run for the tweezers. People are overcommitted. They already have more than they can handle. I respect their grind, and the last thing I want is to add to the burden.

And if I am being really honest—because, hey, evidently that's a side perk in writing this super fun exposé of the deepest parts of my heart—I have been asked to do things I didn't really want to do . . . and I helped out of obligation. The sad thing is, the recipients probably felt a sense of duty coming from me and not a feeling of kindness.

If that spoke to you, I am so sorry.
I should have loved you better.

On the flip side, though, while I don't like asking for help, I generally love to offer it. When I'm not feeling selfish, I consider myself a helper, a giver. As a parent, I wanted our kids to be givers in a world of takers. Here's some biblical truth that's always resonated with me, something I encouraged our kids to understand from early on:

"For God loves a cheerful giver."
(2 Corinthians 9:7)

Confession: this was especially part of our conversations when I asked them to help around the house and they wondered if they'd get an extra allowance. I was not that cool of a parent. I wanted our kids to contribute just because that's what happens in families. Focusing on giving cheerfully and how it pleases God was brought up often.

Parents, I know you're wondering:
it worked about 50 percent of the time.

Just like I wanted the kids to give from a cheerful place, I want God to love what He sees in my heart when I help others. To me, sharing His love with a hurting world is a tangible way to thank Him for His gift of grace. I could never thank God enough for saving me from my destructive ways, but it feels great to try.

While we don't need to earn His love, we can say thank you.

"For it is by grace you have been saved, through faith—
and this is not from yourselves, it is the gift of God—
not by works, so that no one can boast."
(Ephesians 2:8–9)

As a church youth leader, I often shared with my students the joy that comes with living lives that shout "Thank You" to God. We talked about it again and again.

My students were either
super tired of hearing me say this, or
so distracted wondering if we had any nachos left,
they are hearing it for the first time in this book.

Helping others as a means of thanking God is why giving feels so amazing. It fills our joy buckets to lighten the load that people carry. Giving an ounce of support can help a person lose a pound of burden. It is right and good to do life together. No one was meant to live completely alone.

"And let us consider how we may spur one another on toward love
and good deeds, not giving up on meeting together."
(Hebrews 10:24–25)

When we share the load, we help people realize they are seen and heard, because they matter.

Maybe you are also the type of person who finds joy in being there for—and with—others.

Are giving and helping on your Joy Bucket List?

We all know, on some level, it feels good to feel good.

There it is, my unscientific philosophy for spreading joy.
It feels good to feel good.
If you follow me on social media for more than five minutes,
you'll hear me say this.

In my opinion, what doesn't feel good is
- being labeled as "looking for attention,"
- bringing other people down,
- worrying the people I care about,
- making others feel sorry for me,
- and at the bottom of the list, making people feel less optimistic about their own situations when they compare and realize they have it worse.

That's the real kicker—the biggest reason I didn't want to share my struggles or ask for help when I was injured. I could share the little things but not this. If someone with a more difficult situation heard me complaining about bumping my head and said, "What does she have to complain about? She could have it as bad as I do," what purpose would it serve?

So, when I got a mild TBI (traumatic brain injury) from skiing, I hid my pain from the world and tried to do most things myself. Other than my family, a few close friends, and some paid professionals, no one knew how I was really feeling. I did not want them to know. I did the best I could to avoid the world and its questions. I didn't even want the church prayer team to know.

It is still hard to share my hurts. Even now, I can't get through writing this easily. My stomach is churning. I just realized I am holding my breath. I keep stepping away, checking social media, actively seeking distractions.

Gosh, thirty-two new emails.

It's hard to share what hurting felt like, because

    A. it didn't feel good at all, and

    B. I didn't feel like I had any right to complain.

The truth is, symptoms from my concussion made me feel awful. Like roadkill. A road pancake.

In college, I became friends with an exchange student from Japan.
She loved learning American slang and took great joy in declaring that
every dead raccoon on the side of the road was "road pizza."
Yoko Mochizuki, if I had known your name was the Japanese version of
Jane Doe, I would've saved your address.

Empathy is everything, and experiencing a concussion myself means I'll never take people's concussion diagnoses lightly again. If you have a head injury, I will jump at the chance to be there for you. I now know that having a TBI can make a person look normal but feel completely helpless.

Here's something I learned: never tell someone who admits
they are hurting in any way that they "look fine."
It minimizes their pain and makes them not want to open up.
As rarely as I shared about my TBI, I heard "you look fine"
enough to consider carrying a Sharpie so I could ask people
if they wanted to "sign my cast."
A compassionate "I'm so sorry you're hurting"
would have landed better.

In an instant, my head injury forced me to stop doing most of my normal activities just to minimize the pain. I went from living fully—aiming my bike for the puddles and climbing up on the roof of my house to relax and pray—to merely surviving and just getting through the day.

Concussions make people emotional, and I was no exception.

My tear ducts were already the most muscular part of my body.
They are ripped.
They didn't need more workouts.

Because I couldn't talk about it without crying, I kept quiet and smiled so no one knew. Since I felt I couldn't share my feelings, I learned to dodge questions. When people asked how I was, I gave brief, nondescript answers and came back with questions about their lives. I got good at redirecting the conversation away from myself. Anything to keep me out of the focus.

If you notice someone regularly answering questions with questions,
there is a good chance they are hurting.
"How are you?" makes "Fine, how are you?" an easy answer.
Instead, ask something to help them release
some of their inner struggle, like
"What's been the toughest part of today so far?"

Life was messy. I felt broken and screwed up and alone, but because I could walk and talk, I didn't think I had a right to feel bad. I was grateful. I didn't want anyone to think I was looking for attention.

Social interactions—a massive source of joy for me—had to be extremely minimal. Regular conversations made me feel dizzy, unable to follow a train of thought, in need of hearing things restated over and over, and exhausted from trying to connect the mental dots while pretending I was okay. Most group gatherings were out of the question.

Doing much thinking at all made my brain feel like it was being squeezed in a vise. You know, those workbench clamps that relentlessly smoosh the daylights out of the thing in the middle? My brain was the thing. The pressure was horrendous.

To make matters worse, my concussion kept me from sleeping deeply. It meant sleeping just below the surface of consciousness. I was already a light sleeper. Now anything that woke me up during the night meant I'd end up lying awake for hours, trying to go back to sleep. I would pray for other people, count my blessings, do deep breathing exercises, journal in the pitch black (with horrible handwriting), recite one word of the Lord's Prayer with each breath, anything to go back to sleep. It rarely worked. The next day I would function slowly, living in a fog, feeling like a zombie with road pizza for a brain.

There were times when having a head injury felt like being hit with a steamroller. There were other times when it felt like living in a blender: life was swirly and out of control.

The word *swirly* brings up a distinct memory of trying to make dinner for my family. I wanted so badly to contribute and do a normal thing like follow a new recipe.

Before my injury I could cook dinner, wash the dishes, create the next week's grocery list, put away the laundry, and place an Amazon order at the same time.

In this particular experience, I struggled hard to complete the cooking steps in order. I couldn't remember where I was in the process or make sense of what came next. Attempting to learn something new made me feel all swirly and confused, unsure, like I was trapped in a KitchenAid on full speed.

Rick was right there, wanting to help me. I wanted to do it myself. I could tell the whole thing made him feel sad.

I finished the recipe, but I felt exasperated, teary-eyed, and stupid.

The truth is, I have needed to learn how to ask for help for years. This time, I thought I would be rescued by a healed brain before I actually had to ask. When I was at the emergency room on the day of my skiing accident, I remember being dumbfounded when the ER docs predicted that it would take seven to ten days to resume normal activities. I thought, *Holy cow, I can't do anything for a week? How am I going to ask for help for seven days?* They basically advised, "If it hurts, don't do it." I could not imagine putting my business and personal life on hold for that long, but my head hurt so badly, I had no choice. I reluctantly agreed to get mental and physical rest and avoid exposure to screens, lights, loud sounds, and additional head injuries. My plan was to spend a week lying down in the dark while doing any bits of work I could get away with. I needed to let my brain heal and somehow continue to make work progress on my own. I figured it would be slow, but I wouldn't allow myself to get overwhelmed because it would only last for a week. Worst-case scenario, it would take ten days. I could survive that long.

I didn't want to bother anyone, so I tried to keep my pain to myself unless someone asked. For the first few days, I hardly got out of bed. I did ask to have my laptop brought in our room but found it hard to do much computer work at all. The pain was intense, and I couldn't comprehend written or spoken words without really concentrating, which hurt. Even with the brightness of my screen dimmed down, just trying to think made my head hurt. Writing basic emails was too much.

I made my phone's background black, but looking at websites and sending texts were still out of the question. I learned to use voice texting and stopped caring about the translation errors. Alone in my dark room, I made a new discovery: I could send audio messages so I didn't feel completely isolated from the world.

This might make the young people in your life crazy, but did you know you can skip typing and send an audio message by hitting the microphone button on the following applications?

- Facebook Messenger
- LinkedIn
- Snapchat
- Instagram
- Text messages (as long as you are sending from iPhone to iPhone or Android to Android)

This saved me so many times. And it allowed for
better connection anyway. Joy!

I was glad to be able to send and receive messages, but my loved ones did not like the idea of me trying to do any work. Like, any work. Out of love, they were checking in with me constantly about how much I was doing or not doing. It felt good to be cared for, but it was hard to listen to their reminders of what the doctors had said.

I did not want to think about what the doctors had said.

As a solopreneur, no work meant no progress; progress had to come from me, or it wasn't happening. I had to keep trying. At the time, I didn't realize it but the pressure I put on myself to do it all created an unhealthy mindset of self-sufficiency. My belief system told me it was a trap the enemy of my soul set for me, one that I walked right into.

Kelly Clarkson is belting out the chorus of
"Miss Independent" in my mind right now.
Wow. I never saw myself in that one before.

How could I forget that the business was the Lord's to begin with? Did I not believe that He would carry it? Did I stop trusting in His timing and provision altogether? While I was grateful my injury wasn't worse and it felt like I was thanking Him for that fact nonstop, the whole idea of submitting my work life to Him wasn't happening because I was afraid He would put it on pause, and seven days of pausing was long enough. It was a trust issue from the start. I wrongly believed it was all on my shoulders. I knew better, but I did it anyway.

The stress added to the headaches, dizziness, mental blur, and inability to stay asleep. I was overwhelmed from focusing on my own inabilities . . . without focusing on who God was. More nasty self-sufficiency. More feelings of failure. More symptoms. What a trap. It was a heck of a way to spend a week off.

I'd like to say I hit the seven-day mark and the Lord magically healed my head. But then there wouldn't be a book. The truth is, the pain wasn't improving. I tried to be understanding, but it was a shock.

There would be more of this? Are you kidding?

Resigned to accept the fact that it could take the whole ten days, I tried to relax. Soon enough I would be okay. It wouldn't last much longer.

Finally, I hit the magical ten-day milestone. I was hoping to wake up pain free, ready to live life and celebrate. The roof was waiting. So was my bike. I didn't care that it was February, still the heart of winter.

But my head still wasn't better. At all.

Was I feeling joy? No, at this point I was feeling anger. Frustration. Disappointment. Shame. I had put all of my eggs into the basket of real life returning, and it felt like the whole basket was smashed on the floor, eggs everywhere, just like little brains on drugs from 1980s TV.

I was reminded of when Missy was born two days after her due date. For months we prepared for one date, sharing it excitedly every time we were asked. When that date passed, and we still weren't holding our baby, we didn't know how to feel. It was the same feeling of . . . *wait, what?*

Side note:
The whole "protect others by keeping my feelings to myself"
thing is exploding in my mind right now.
There are so many couples who have lost children,
who would give anything for the two-day delay I complained about.
I am sorry for your pain and don't intend any insensitivity.
I hope you'll understand why I shared my story.

The time had come to accept reality: the ER doctors were a little off, and even though the CT scans and MRIs came back clear, this concussion was worse than it originally seemed. It left me feeling adrift with no land in sight, not knowing how long it would take to get my life back.

Which direction should I swim?
Would I drown altogether if I didn't know what to aim for?

The "how much longer?" questions others asked didn't help because I didn't have the answers. On the inside I felt like a failure, wondering if I had caused the continued pain by trying to do too much work. Again, a trap of the enemy, one I fell for hook, line, and sinker. I felt like a mental and emotional train wreck.

Because I wasn't healing, my family doctor ordered another MRI. I was hopeful they might find something fixable.

Now I am relieved they didn't.

As is usually the case with mild TBIs, there was nothing to show. Thankfully, I was referred to a concussion specialist and thought, *This guy will fix me. He will know what I can do to get better. This will be my turning point.*

My specialist listened to my story, heard my questions, and tried to reassure me my brain would heal. He prescribed medication for pain management and sleep. He advised me to take it easy but gave me permission to do 25 percent of my usual workload if it didn't hurt my head.

It did.

Here I was, excited to have permission to try, chomping at the bit to get stuff done, and I couldn't even do a quarter of it. I had to learn really quickly which one thing to focus on each morning before the pain got bad. It was crazy to go from doing all of the things to doing one thing a day. One.

Because I was too stubborn to ask for help, my work pile grew and so did my stress. My family helped tremendously around the house without being asked, but could they have helped run my business? They would have tried, but it would have been so mentally taxing to explain what needed to be done. Could I have hired an assistant? In a perfect world where helping jobs are paid appropriately, yes. Could I have asked my industry friends to help out? Actually, yes: my entrepreneur friends would have understood, and many would have jumped in. But they were running their own businesses, and I didn't want to add to their loads. I didn't ask. Stuff piled up.

So, other than coaching my clients and speaking on virtual stages, which I refused to cancel even though they took everything I had for the whole day, my business basically came to a screeching halt. Not asking for help made me the modern-day subject of the well-known proverb,

"Pride goes before destruction, a haughty spirit before a fall."
(Proverbs 16:18)

One lesson the Lord surely wanted me to learn: it's good to ask for help. But I wasn't ready to learn it because I thought I knew more than He did.

"Whoever trusts in his own mind is a fool,
but he who walks in wisdom will be delivered."
(Proverbs 28:26 ESV)

Thankfully, some friends knew what was going on and did not wait for me to ask them for help. This meant that my family had relief when

- Zonya prayed with me often and brought us delicious, healing dinners so many times, I lost track.
- Judie prayed with me by listening to my voice messages and replying with her own. We did this several times.

Listening to her peaceful voice soothed me beyond words.

- Bob learned that apples and cocoa are good for the brain and sent a whole box of chocolate-covered apples. They were amazing and a wonderful reminder that I wasn't alone.
- Rachel checked in often, always validating my feelings. It was so helpful.
- Julie, a new grandma, brought her growing family over just to fill my joy bucket with the smells, sights, and sounds of a new baby. As hard as it was to focus on the conversation, being with them really lifted my spirits.
- Roger made me laugh by sending uplifting messages and funny movie clips. Rog, you missed your calling as a movie critic. "I feel the need . . . the need for speed."

I know that many others would have helped if they had known. But here's the thing I realize now: by not sharing, I never gave them the chance to. Eventually, when I was able to talk about my situation without crying or wanting to crawl in a hole, I got the same answer, again and again:

"I wish I had known. I had no idea. I would have helped you."

The true sadness on their faces made me realize that by not sharing my struggle, by not asking for help, I robbed them of the ability to love me. I was trying to protect them, and in the end, I hurt them.

Clearly, this was not what God would want. How does my life say thank you to God when I don't accept the love He was offering through others? And what if other people wanted to shout thank you to the Lord with their lives and I was blocking them from doing it? What does that say about me?

Looking back, I totally understand why I felt so lonely.

It was a pride problem. My pride kept me from feeling the presence of God through the majority of people in my life. Believing I should do it all myself meant that I didn't give Him the chance to show up through others.

Here's a question that begs asking: where was the joy in all of my self-sufficiency?

The thing is, I am surrounded by cheerful givers—people God loves, right? By not asking for their help, I ended up stealing their joy. My actions made the very people that God loves feel unloved . . . by me.

Here's the big question that brings us back to the beginning of the chapter:

Q: Why is it so hard to ask for help?

A: Because the enemy wants us to believe it's better to do everything ourselves.

The way I see it, because he is a joy-stealing, scum-sucking dog, Satan will try to convince us to think we can do it on our own. Isolating and believing we are self-sufficient is not in line with God's character at all. God is very much about relationship. The urge to be self-sufficient has got to come from the enemy of our souls, because there's no way it's coming from the Lord. After all, if we can do all things, if we don't need help, why would we need God? When we keep our hurts in and refuse to let other people truly know and help us, the enemy wins the battle.

God loves cheerful givers. I want to do the same. I'll try to give them opportunities to put His love into action, because it will bring them joy. Even if it means asking for help.

Oh God, please help me ask for help.

Messy Joy Spill-Your-Guts Journal Questions:

1. Do you ask for help as often as you should? Why or why not?

2. When you consider asking for help, what thoughts come up?

3. Give examples of the last three times you asked for help.

4. Would you call yourself a cheerful giver? If not, what's getting in your way?

5. What message does your life shout to God and others?

6. When you help other people, what effect does it have on your joy bucket? Why might this be? (If it fills your joy bucket, have you added "helping others" to your list?)

7. Do you let people help you? What might this say about you?

8. When you are hurting, would you describe yourself as an open book, a closed chapter, or something else? Why?

9. When someone asks how you are and you're in a difficult period, how do you reply? Where does this type of response come from?

10. What questions can you ask instead of "How are you?" when you suspect someone might be in pain? What do you wish people would ask you?

11. When have you trusted the Lord to carry you? Explain what that felt like and how God showed up. On the flip side, share a time you didn't ask God for help or didn't ask Him soon enough. What happened?

12. How do you handle disappointment when things don't happen when or how you'd like?

13. What lies does the enemy tell you to keep you from trusting God fully?

14. Where does pride show up in your life? What effect does that have?

15. Self-sufficiency is a tool the enemy uses to keep us from relying on God. As this thought settles, what feelings come up for you?

16. What are some of the most helpful things people have ever done for you? Did you ask, or were they done without your asking?

17. What effect, if any, does this chapter have on your views of asking for help?

18. What does accepting help from others say about you? About your view of God?

CHAPTER 5

Where Is Joy When Life Brings More Questions Than Answers?

ere's a fun question: What will people say about you at your funeral?

Told you it was fun.

But seriously, what will they say?

I hope to be remembered as someone who was upbeat and wanted to help others. Someone who was positive and not only saw the glass half full, but who was thankful the glass even existed.

When I had a TBI, there were days when I didn't feel this way at all. If you want to know the truth, there were days when I projected a positive outlook to others but secretly felt like my life was falling apart. I was hiding a mess. I felt like smashing the glass.

I am glad I didn't die in that state of mind. It would have given people at my funeral every reason to say I was inauthentic and hiding the truth.

Here I was, a joy coach, struggling to find joy. I spoke of it often and helped others find it throughout my recovery, but my life was not filled with it.

My life was filled with questions. Being filled with questions is not a fun place to be.

Have you ever been there? You've got a question. It's a big one. Before long, thinking about it leads to another big question. And another. Your mind suddenly seems overrun by uncertainty. Even the things that you once knew seem to be unsure. Your brain feels like a glass jar, each question a marble, and marbles keep getting added. The jar is being swirled. With gusto. Soon you're entrenched in a spinning blur of questions, with no end in sight.

This cannot be what God wants for us.

"For God is not the author of confusion, but of peace."
(1 Corinthians 14:33 KJV)

Peace is the exact opposite of the spinning jar.

The question becomes, Who, then, wants us to be confused? Who is spinning the dang thing?

And the follow up question: Why are we listening to that voice anyway?

It's no wonder it's hard to find joy when we are focused on questions. While a good question can get our minds going, too many big ones can leave us feeling anxious, scared, and confused. They can hold us captive and give us anything but peace.

At times, that's exactly where I was: projecting the message of choosing joy, but inwardly anxious, scared, and confused. Of course joy was hard to find. In fact, there were days when being an expert in joy and struggling hard to find it made me feel like a monumental fraud. More on that later.

Don't get me wrong: I knew what brought joy to me. It wasn't about knowing. It was about putting it into practice. About doing.

Thankfully, I had given thought to my personal sources of joy in the years leading up to my accident. I will refer you again to your Joy Bucket List inside the back cover of the book. Do the work now of exploring what brings joy to you. Grow your list. When you need it, it will be there to help you. Trust me on this.

For me, the foundation had been laid, and it was there for me to build on and put to use. Before the accident, I knew that I personally found joy in so many things:

- Making memories with my family
- Getting my hands dirty and helping others in need
- Being grateful
- Childlike thinking
- Exploring purpose
- Practicing mindfulness
- Meeting my self-care needs
- Remembering meaningful memories
- Connecting to people, especially any who were different from me
- Moving my body in any number of ways
- Digging into my faith
- Learning about others' beliefs
- Deepening relationships with people I love
- Living spontaneously and veering off the expected path
- Getting lost in the wonder of nature
- Letting music stir my soul and take me over
- Learning and accomplishing new things
- Interacting with animals of (almost) all types (Confession: I'm not a fan of sloths. Gasp!)
- Organizing and improving the functionality of things
- Stretching my comfort zone with new experiences
- Feeling heard, seen, and valued, and offering this gift to others
- A tear-jerking belly laugh
- Being generous or witnessing generosity in action
- Stillness and quiet rest
- Contributing to something bigger than myself

Side note: Do any of these things bring joy to you as well?
Maybe they spark other ideas? Turn to your Joy Bucket List
and add anything that belongs there.
I'll wait here.

When I hit my head, my list was long. That meant I had choices when things were beyond my control. I could rely on several things to help me feel like myself. If I could give you any advice, it would be to grow your list often. Do not limit your thinking. Pay attention to what sparks joy in you, and be sure to write it down. Even if you don't have *Messy Joy* with you when the idea bubbles up, make a note in your phone or on scrap paper to add it to your Joy Bucket List later.

I'd like to expand on a few sources of joy that I really relied on, especially when I was filled with questions.

Being Grateful

During my recovery, one of the most reliable sources of joy to come in clutch was gratitude. A sign on our kitchen wall reads "There is always, always something to be thankful for," and even on my lowest days it was true. I could always find reasons to express gratitude.

I was thankful for having my loyal family by my side day and night. These saints (there is no better word) were so committed to walking with me through the mess. I don't know where I would be without my husband, kids, parents, and sister. They never made me feel bad for not being able to do things. They checked in on me and let me know they cared. They jumped at the chance to help. Just their presence made me feel more like me. Honestly, the minute they entered the room or sent me a message, gratitude welled up. My tear ducts were working overtime to keep up.

I was so thankful my injury wasn't worse. So thankful! The reality was that I could have been—but wasn't—paralyzed in an instant. It happens all the time. In the CDC's report entitled "Prevalence and

Causes of Paralysis, United States, 2013" (which appears to be the most recent study), the leading causes of paralysis were stroke and spinal cord injury. Who am I to say how close I was to a spinal cord injury? I'll never know. All I know is I remembered what it felt like to land on the back of my head from super high up and how I couldn't move my head with that hard plastic collar on while we waited for test results. Now I recognize that a certain slight bend in the neck could have been devastating. I was so grateful for the promise that my injury would heal, knowing this is not the result many others have lived with. Throughout my recovery I prayed for people who had it worse, and I continue to do so.

Gratitude overflowed knowing God was at work. God was still good even if my situation wasn't, and He was very much alive and well despite my setback.

"The Lord is good to all; he has compassion on all he has made."
(Psalm 145:9)

I saw Him at work everywhere. In fact, I felt a closeness to Him like never before.

"The Lord is close to the brokenhearted
and saves those who are crushed in spirit."
(Psalm 34:18)

Even when I was at my lowest—whether that was in the ER, or later when I feared the injury was permanent, or somewhere in between—He was with me, and I never doubted that for a minute. I saw Him in big and small things, like in the miracle of being able to inhale and exhale without trying—have you ever thought about that? How does the oxygen know where to go? How do the cells know how to utilize it? It's incredible how God designed us to do so much that we rarely slow down to appreciate. When life is forced to pause, time for appreciation becomes suddenly available. I felt God's love in the beautiful laughter of family and friends, in the wholeness I felt through so many loving embraces, in the sleep that I did get to experience, and in so many other aspects of life. The Lord's steadfast presence brought me so much gratitude and so much joy.

Getting Lost in the Wonder of Nature

Thankfully, our beautiful world is filled with incredible detail, and it brought me joy. I had all the time in the world just to appreciate the awesomeness of creation, like the way the clouds were so varied within the same sky—oh, how I love the shapes, sizes, textures, and colors of clouds!—and the way they gently blew out of view, disappearing into nothing. *Wow! How did they do that and where did they go?* I found joy in the tiniest details. I remember being amazed by the way the icicles formed outside our kitchen window, reflecting the world around them like tiny mirror sticks. Months later I was drawn in by the many vivid shades of yellow on a dandelion growing up through a crack in the sidewalk.

Thank You, God, for being such an artistic show-off! All of your yellows are rich and energizing. Why do we label dandelions as weeds? You were so good when you made those!

When bright sunlight caused headaches, the richness of a dark sky seemed extra beautiful. Oh, the vastness of the night sky! Visible stars were an added bonus. They seemed to hold promise and remind me that God was capable of so much I would never know how to understand.

"The whole earth is filled with awe at your wonders; where morning dawns, where evening fades, you call forth songs of joy."
(Psalm 65:8)

I found joy in the feel of the wind whooshing and announcing its winter presence, the sound of our cat Mickey's aging but always-present purr, and the cold snow on my face while I slowly trudged around trying to keep up with our Goldendoodle. Molly never seemed to lack energy.

Helping Others in Need

Another source of joy that held true throughout my recovery was being able to help others. I needed so badly to feel like I was still making a difference, that time wasn't completely wasting away. I spoke to virtual audiences every time I was asked without regard to repercussions, wanting to share a message of hope with anyone who might need one. It may have wiped me out for the rest of the day, but I gave it all I had, gratefully. I pray that each of the thirteen audiences I had the privilege of speaking to were served in some way.

One time I faced my fear of facing crowds and read the liturgy at church when asked. I tried so hard to pronounce the words right and act normal, but some words tripped me up, especially "contemplative," which was in the reading a couple of times. The whole time I was in front of the congregation, I held my breath, fearing people would know something was wrong and ask why. I was still hiding my secret. I pretty much bolted out of there the second the service ended, feeling like a cat in a display cage. But I was grateful to help.

I was also able to help a friend who was going through a very scary time. At first I reached out to her for help because she had suffered a severe concussion years earlier, and I needed someone to tell me I wasn't crazy for needing so long to recover (thank You for helping me in this way, God). In the midst of our ongoing conversation, which spanned months, her cancer came back. It put me in a position to be there for her and hear what was on her heart. I tried to give her a safe space to be real. As the Holy Spirit led, I sent her prayers with the audio recording option. Her heart's language is music, and the Lord brought to mind several songs to share with her. I couldn't take her cancer away, but I could listen and speak truth into her fears when she wanted to hear it.

While I would love to say joy was present throughout my recovery, the truth is, there were many times finding it was a struggle. I knew what I needed to fill my joy bucket. Obtaining it was a different story. Many of my sources of joy seemed out of reach. They seemed to be on hold. My marbles were spinning day and night. I was filled with questions:

- How could I find joy making memories with my family when simple conversations left me feeling clueless and teary?
- Would I ever be physically strong enough to serve on a mission trip again? How could I swing a pick axe, give a child a piggyback ride, or pour concrete again?
- When self-care equates to having fun and adventure, how would I ever meet that need?
- How could I connect with people when I hid my gaze so they wouldn't see the uncertainty and fear in my eyes?
- Would moving my body always make my head pound? Would the fun override the pain?
- How could I dig into my faith when the thinking required to read and listen to the Bible were exhausting and I could hardly bear to face the crowd at church?
- Would anyone want to deepen their relationship with me when I felt sluggish, swirly, and boring? Wouldn't they find better things to do?

The list went on and on. Questions spun through my mind day and night. It was difficult to slow them down and be present in the moment. I felt like the jar would never be at rest.

This began what I can only describe as a war in my head. And looking back, I am sure this brought delight to the enemy of my soul.

"The thief comes only to steal and kill and destroy."
(John 10:10)

The jerk was trying to steal my focus away from the goodness of God, and I fell for it. I fell prey to allowing myself to ask all the questions I wanted, and my questions fed more questions. I was trapped in fear and uncertainty.

I wondered, How could a joy coach not find joy? What right did I have to help others if I couldn't help myself? Was I even qualified to be a joy coach at this point? There were times when I questioned the validity of my calling so much, I almost gave up on it. I feared my work was garbage, and I owed a whole lot of people apologies. I seriously considered closing my business for good, because I didn't know if I could help other people when my own life felt so fractured and fake.

I also began to question my understanding of joy itself. Was my philosophy on happiness and joy wrong all along? If happiness was circumstantial and joy was a way of being, as I believed before the accident, why couldn't I always be joyful, despite my circumstances? Why did I need certain situations—like the absence of concussion symptoms—to bring me joy sometimes? Did that not make joy circumstantial? It was so confusing that it hurt my head to think about. But it was a question I came back to again and again because having a deeper understanding would not only help me, it would help me help others.

In addition, new questions ran through my mind that were so scary, I continually tried to shove them back down and silence them.

What if I needed to learn to find joy in silence?
In rest?
In solitude?
And what if I needed to do this forever?

These "new and improved" sources of joy were so opposite of my norm. Choosing them felt like settling. They felt inauthentic to who

I was. While I do find joy in moments of mindfulness and stillness, I didn't want to live the rest of my life that way. I am the girl who jumps up to dance when "Gettin' Jiggy Wit It" plays on the jukebox, does cannonballs in the lake with her clothes on, and has picnics in the January snow. How could I feel truly joyful when so many of my sources of joy might be permanently off the table?

Thankfully, God, the author of peace, was there. He did not intend for me to drown in uncertainty. He gently reminded me of advice that I had given to others and made it clear that it was applicable to me as well. When our kids were uncertain about something in their lives, I had shared this advice with them. I had also freely discussed it with others who were filled with questions, like teens in my youth groups with big decisions to make, friends going through personal struggles, nutrition clients with eating disorders, and senior citizens living daily with dementia.

The advice I needed to be reminded of was this: When life holds more questions than answers, focus on what you do know for sure.

Read that again if you need to.

So, what do you know for sure? What do you know to be true without fail? What does not change? Remind yourself of that, dwell on it, give thanks for it, and let it bring you peace. Specifically, my questions were quieted when I followed the wisdom of Philippians 4:8:

"Finally, brothers and sisters, whatever is true, whatever is noble, whatever is right, whatever is pure, whatever is lovely, whatever is admirable—if anything is excellent or praiseworthy— think about such things."

There was so much in each of the above categories that I could focus on to slow the marbles in my mind. Whatever you are facing, it's not more uncertain than these things, which are certain. They will win every time.

When you are filled with too many questions to count, get started on the "whatever is true" part. Ask yourself to name an example of truth. How many can you name?

Move on. What or who in your life is noble?

Am I the only one who rarely uses the word noble?
What does noble even mean?
My Bible dictionary defines it as "possessing high moral qualities."
I am going to stop thinking of it in terms of kings and queens because my circle is filled with so many everyday
people who are truly noble.

As you think about the world around you, what is right? How does it make you feel to think about the things that are right?

Name some things that are truly pure. How wonderful to dwell on them!

If you were to think about what is lovely, what comes to mind? There may not be enough time in the day to list them all.

What or whom do you admire? Why?

When we think about all these things—not to mention the things that are excellent and praiseworthy—we recognize that they are blessings, and we cannot help but give thanks to the Giver. It's comforting to go there, because what we know for sure is, if God made these good things that mean so much to us, He can definitely help us with the uncertainties we face.

As you retrain your brain to stop the mental madness and focus on the truths in Philippians 4:8, expect some pushback. It won't be easy at first. Satan doesn't want us to remember the truth about God. All the more reason to keep doing it! It's okay. It will get easier. Soon it will be the preferred route.

And for bonus joy points, focus on what we know to be unquestionable of God:

- God is good (You're right, "all the time").
- God is able.
- God is loving.
- God is merciful.
- God is faithful.
- God is forgiving.
- God is creative.
- God is unpredictable and full of surprises.
- God is unchanging.
- God is kind.
- God is strong.
- God is so much smarter than we are.
- And God is so much more.

When questions get spinning in your mind, slow them down with a long list of peaceful truths as directed in Philippians 4:8. Why? When life brings more questions than answers, focusing on what we know to be true brings joy!

Messy Joy Spill-Your-Guts Journal Questions:

1. Describe a time when you felt you had more questions than answers. What was happening? How did it make you feel?
2. As you think about that time in your life, what did you find to be helpful?
3. Would you say that times of uncertainty tend to bring you joy? What else do they bring you?
4. How have you relied on God during times of confusion?
5. What has God taught you about Himself during those times?
6. If you were to describe peace to someone, how would you describe it?
7. Is there a connection between peace and joy?
8. Elaborate on a time you distinctly knew that the Lord was blessing you with peace.
9. As God is the author of peace, what would you say Satan is the author of? Why does he want you to experience that? How does it affect the peace in your life?
10. What are some of the ways the enemy shows up in your life? How can you combat him?
11. Are there any scriptures in particular that you keep (or would like to keep) tucked in your heart to ward off the enemy when he strikes?

12. Have you ever projected one image while inwardly feeling the opposite? What effect did it have on you? What effect did it have on the amount of joy in your life?

13. If you were to try to put your top three sources of joy in order right now, what might they be?

14. When was the last time you really made quality time for these joys? What effect did it have on you?

15. Where can you make note of new things that bring you joy until you can record them in your Joy Bucket List?

16. Describe the most joyful experience you've had related to nature, if you've experienced this. Go into detail, as if sharing your experience with someone who has never experienced the same. Why did it have an impact on you?

17. What effect does helping others in need have on your joy bucket? Why might this be?

18. Have you ever felt you had a war going on in your head? How were you able to bring it to an end? What advice would you give?

19. The next time you are faced with uncertainty, what truths do you want to have ready and waiting to cling to? Why might these truths be especially helpful?

20. Take time to pray about the words in Philippians 4:8. As you do, what examples come to mind? Spend time pondering these things. What effect does this reflection have on your joy level?

21. As you look back on your life, what words would you use to describe God to someone who has never been in relationship with Him?

22. How does thinking about the certainties of God affect the confidence you have in His ability to help in difficult times? How does this tie into experiencing joy when life's messy?

CHAPTER 6

Am I Too Afraid to Trust You, Lord?

W hen a fire truck passes by with its lights flashing and horn blaring, what thoughts do you have? It's such a billboard for "Someone's life is changing right this second" that I often find myself praying for the victims, first responders, and family members to feel the presence of God. God's presence changes everything, and I always thought I was the type of person who would automatically feel it and trust Him in a crisis.

God has shown up throughout my life without fail. He has given me every reason to believe I can rely on Him, no matter what. I'd hear stories of people crumbling under the weight of hardship, and I'd pray that their faith would be strengthened, believing I would have mountains of hope and optimism in their shoes.

Going through my own season of reckoning taught me that even if my faith was strong, fear could be stronger, if I chose to give in to it. It wasn't always about faith; it was often about choice.

As my ten-day TBI recovery goal was tossed aside and replaced by a disappointing ten weeks of continued symptoms, I wasn't feeling very optimistic at all. Nor was I always focusing on God's presence.

Nope. I was a joy coach, at times privately wallowing in despair.

After each virtual appointment with my concussion specialist, my family would call to see if there was any hopeful new information. There wasn't. It was more of the same advice of wait and see. My family continually reinforced what the doctor advised me to do, worrying I was overdoing it. Wait and see. It had been a good seventy days. Seventy. Waiting and seeing were the last things I wanted to do.

The meds that were prescribed didn't seem to help with the symptoms, and the side effects were awful. The accident was in January, and I still wasn't sleeping well or able to do much by Easter. I was losing hope. I continued to wonder if my life would ever get back to normal.

I cried often through my concussion doctor appointments. After faking it with the rest of the world, I felt I needed to be honest with my specialist so he could know the whole story for proper treatment. Maybe if he knew how bad things really were, he would try something different? I feared judgment with every cell I had, but in order to get my life back, I pushed aside my fear and shared everything. Sharing my true symptoms and fears out loud hurt, and I could not stop the tears. The poor guy had to sit through so many Zoom appointments while I spilled my guts and sobbed.

Sorry, dude. I owe you a free joy coaching session.

Even though I was running low on hope at this point, there was enough to make me want to keep trying. I attempted to do what I was instructed to do and waited. I (mostly) rested, avoided all alcohol, was careful not to hit my head, tried to sleep, took the meds, and dealt with the side effects . . . and I still didn't heal. I knew the time was coming to try something different, but what? It had already been ten times longer than the ER doc's predictions, and I was desperate to get my life back, though I secretly doubted it would ever get better.

If I am being really honest, all of this waiting fed into an enormous battle brewing in my heart about trusting in God's timing.

**"But do not forget this one thing, dear friends:
With the Lord a day is like a thousand years, and a thousand years
are like a day. The Lord is not slow in keeping his promise,
as some understand slowness."**
(2 Peter 3:8–9)

That's really cool, but I did not want to wait a thousand years. I knew that God could heal my injury. Of this I had zero doubt. God, in His perfect time, could certainly make me whole again. What I didn't know was if He would . . . on Earth. *Could* and *would* are tremendously different. God never promised anyone a life free of pain.

Did He promise you a life free of pain?
I don't know what book you're reading, but that's not in my Bible.

What He did promise was to never leave us, no matter what.

**"It is the LORD who goes before you. He will be with you; He will
not leave you or forsake you. Do not fear or be dismayed."**
(Deuteronomy 31:8 ESV)

He promised He would always be by our side and fight our battles for us.

"The LORD will fight for you; you need only to be still."
(Exodus 14:14)

As awesome as these promises were, I feared they would mean He would be with me and fight my battles . . . while I adjusted to a permanent new normal. People's lives are changed forever in an instant. It could certainly happen to me, and I needed to accept that fact. So, while I trusted that He would heal me, I was beginning to resign myself to the possibility that His plan to heal me might take place in heaven someday.

The thought brought up many secret fears that ran through my mind day and night:

What if I would never be able to do fun things
with my family without asking for help?
What if simple conversations wouldn't be possible
without dreaming of escaping to quietness?
What if group gatherings would be out of the question from now on and I
couldn't go to Christmas or host a birthday party for my kids?
What if trying to follow a recipe would always leave me feeling swirly and
stupid and I would have to settle for serving PB&Js
and mac and cheese forever?
What if I had to close my business because I couldn't
handle the load? Where would I work?
What if I had to exchange spontaneity for stillness
for the rest of my life?
What if people found out I was faking it and struggling to be joyful in the
trenches? Would I be qualified to be a joy coach?

I didn't share my fears with my family or friends because I didn't want to plant seeds of doubt in anyone else's minds. They thought I was going to get better, and I let them. They were already doing so much extra stuff to help me on top of their own stuff, they didn't need to absorb my fear too. I was determined not to worry them. The only stuff I allowed out of my mouth was positive, upbeat, semi-honest.

As I kept the fears bottled up, you guessed it: my symptoms got worse. All of the yuck—the sleeplessness, confusion, head pain, emotion—it intensified. I felt like such a fake, such a phony, and I was paying the price. I was afraid life would always be like this. I needed to be real, and it needed to happen fast.

Satan was a liar and had convinced me to hole up and isolate in order to protect my loved ones from my fears. I was choosing fear—the enemy's playground—instead of faith, and it was destroying me. God, in His goodness, met me in the ick. The Holy Spirit made it real clear I did have someone I could share my inner garbage with, someone who wouldn't be weighed down or affected at all. I did not have to do this alone, and God reminded me I had talked to this person every week, just not with 100 percent authenticity since the accident. The amazing thing was, this person could help me process my fears and also point me to God as the ultimate source of hope. It was such a win-win. I could share all the head trash I wanted, and she would redirect me to the one who could carry my burdens with me.

"Come to me, all you who are weary and burdened, and I will give you rest. Take my yoke upon you and learn from me, for I am gentle and humble in heart, and you will find rest for your souls. For my yoke is easy and my burden is light."
(Matthew 11:28–30)

What a relief that God carried my burdens through my Christian counselor.

Of course I have a therapist. I have sought counseling at three different times in my life, and it has been tremendously helpful. I am glad to share this truth because the stigma that is wrongly assigned to people who seek counseling has got to end. Do I believe everyone should have a life coach and a therapist? Not everyone. Mainly the people who are breathing.

The thing is, it is good and godly to heal from things from our past (with the help of counselors) and gain clarity moving forward (with the help of coaches). Therapists and coaches are dynamic duos for people who don't want to remain stuck. Like me.

To find a therapist, click the "Find a Therapist"
tab on Psychology Today's website.
If you'd like help finding a coach, visit the International Coaching
Federation's "Find a Coach" tab. Or reach out to me using the "Contact"
tab at joytotheworldcoaching.com.

So, with God's help, I started sharing my fears in our counseling sessions. All of them.

Thank You, God . . . even when I am bullheaded, You are so good!
You helped me get that garbage out of my head, and it felt amazing.

Unloading all that stuff took me back to the day I first became Korah's counseling client, telling her, "I am going to keep you busy for a long, long time." Little did I know.

Flashback: On the way home from my very first counseling session with Korah, I got to live a dream. I got to play in the water from a fire hydrant that was being flushed into the street. It was too exciting to pass up, and I highly recommend it as a joy boost, unless you are on your way to therapy,
in which case you may be
analyzed . . . differently.

My therapist was so helpful with all my questions about recovery. We spent many therapy sessions digging into the chaos in my mind. It was a huge relief to be able to be honest without worrying it would affect someone else. I could finally let some of it go.

In addition to listening and asking questions that helped me dissect my fears, she encouraged me to share my fears honestly with the Lord in prayer. He could handle the actual feelings I had been holding back. I did not need to hide them from Him . . . and I couldn't have even if I wanted to.

"You know when I sit and when I rise;
you perceive my thoughts from afar."
(Psalm 139:2)

She was right. It brought me so much relief to tell God what I was truly afraid of. There was so much.

I wouldn't want to be God, would you?
Thank You, Lord, for being God so I can quit trying.

Opening up about my real feelings allowed the scales of fear and faith to tip just a bit, and faith was winning at last. Even though He knew my innermost thoughts, just admitting them in prayer brought me so much comfort, because I knew I could trust God with the deepest parts of my heart. Sharing my whole self somehow allowed me to let go of the scariest parts.

And here's the best part: in sharing, I found peace that God would get me through. He would be my rock. Even if my brain never healed on Earth, being close to God would bring me joy. Yes, joy!

"When anxiety was great within me,
your consolation brought me joy."
(Psalm 94:19)

My joy wouldn't be temporary circumstantial happiness because God Himself would always be present, and He would never, never change.

"For I the Lord do not change."
(Malachi 3:6 ESV)

The peace that He gave me made me feel we were back on the same side of the field, playing on the same team again. Trusting God fully helped me to find joy . . . joy that could only be found in Him.

> **"May the God of hope fill you with all joy and peace**
> **as you trust in him, so that you may overflow**
> **with hope by the power of the Holy Spirit."**
> *(Romans 15:13)*

Thanks be to God, we can be in pain and have joy at the same time. We do *not* have to wait until the pain ends.

Another huge load off was talking with my therapist about finding purpose in the pain. Little did she know, she was speaking my language, one I temporarily needed an interpreter to speak again. Romans 8:28 always spoke volumes to me. It's all about purpose being present in pain. In fact, it's about goodness in pain . . . because God is involved. The NIV version states:

> **"And we know that in all things God works for the good of those**
> **who love him, who have been called according to his purpose."**
> *(Romans 8:28)*

This passage carries so much weight to me personally, I'd like to dig in. Now it's time for a breakdown.

> *Is anyone else hearing En Vogue?*
> *Sorry, y'all, but they were really good in 1992.*

As we dig into this verse, let's pray that we find a few nuggets of wisdom. Here we go.

"And we know that . . ."

We *know*—not we hope or wonder if. We *know*. No matter how bad it seems, He is who He says He is, and we can be certain of that. Look back: God's track record is solid! He did it then and He'll do it now. We can know.

"in all things . . ."

Nothing is off limits. Our worst experiences, the ones we would never willingly sign up for again, the things we regret, the stuff we hide from the world, memories we wish we could erase with amnesia. The things we would prefer to eat, work, gamble, drink, starve, shop, cut, or shoot up to forget. Even those things.

"God . . ."

It's not up to us. Remember who God is and who we are. As they say, "There is a God. And you are not Him." Thanks be to God! What a relief that we can quit trying and get out of the way.

"works for the good . . ."

Wow! For the good. Our tiny brains could spend years trying to understand the majesty of God's goodness. As a meager starting point, my *Life Application Study Bible Dictionary* defines good as "kind; profitable; excellent; fitting or appropriate; morally right." Google agrees.

I don't know about you, but I'm good with all of my things being used for the good . . .

"of those who love Him . . ."

Oh, Lord, as thickheaded as we—I—can be, we do love You. We are sheep who need a Good Shepherd. Why you let us love You, we will never know. Thank You, God, for letting us love You.

"who have been called according to His purpose . . ."

Are we living for ourselves, God? Oh, Lord, You have called us to be Yours and Yours alone! Help us to live according to Your purpose for our lives. It's so much better than anything we can dream up on our own.

"And we know that in all things God works for the good of those who love him, who have been called according to his purpose."
(Romans 8:28)

So much meat in so few words.

I've shared the hope of Romans 8:28 with so many struggling friends who wanted to find purpose in their pain. I believed it with all my heart for them. The time had come to really appreciate the fact that Romans 8:28 applied to me as well. God could use this head injury for His purpose. He could use it for good.

Of course, I had to wonder what God would use it for. What good would He make come from it? Would it affect my loved ones? A stranger? Me? It would be wonderful to know. It would be fun!

Wondering what the good was reminded me of all the aha moments I had driving in the 1990s, listening to radio broadcasts about good coming in the end. I always loved Paul Harvey's *The Rest of the Story* episodes.

If you are old enough, you just heard Paul Harvey say, "And now you know . . . the rest of the story."

I remember driving during my lunch hour with Paul Harvey on my car radio, hoping the static would hold off so I could hear the end, hanging on every word. It was great hearing how things worked out for good, no matter how rough people's situations were. I couldn't get enough.

It dawned on me that now I was tuning in to hear how my own story would end, as told by the same God who created Paul Harvey. But God wasn't just telling my story; He was writing it. This meant guaranteed goodness. Dwelling on the possibilities of the good He could use my head injury for brought even more joy to my messed-up life.

But strangely, letting go of having to know the outcome also brought me joy. When I put myself in perspective compared to the Lord God Almighty, what right do I have to be privy to His wonders at all? It's laughable!

> **"When I consider your heavens,**
> **the work of your fingers,**
> **the moon and the stars,**
> **which you have set in place,**
> **what is mankind that you are mindful of them,**
> **human beings that you care for them?"**
> *(Psalm 8:3–4)*

God is God, and I am me. God would do what He said He would, even if He didn't fill me in on the rest of the story. He said He would use it for good. God works miracles every day that I know nothing of, but that doesn't make them any less awesome and real.

As an example, every time I visit the ocean, I am amazed at two things:

- the power of the water, and
- the way God makes the waves roll even when I know nothing of them.

Oh, how I love the ocean! Sunsets over the water are the stuff dreams are made of. All the rich, vivid colors mixing on display above the sights and sounds and smells of the crashing water makes me feel fully alive. I can hardly believe God lets me experience moments of basking in His glory like that.

Fun fact: the purple and orange all over my website were intentionally chosen brand colors to remind me of the beautiful ocean sunsets that bring me so much joy.
Should you add dwelling on the richness of color to your Joy Bucket List?

But the thing is, when I leave the ocean and can't hear the waves anymore, they are still powerful and still rolling. I don't have to experience them for myself. In the same way, God could use my TBI for incredible good that I might never be aware of. He could use it to bless someone who needed to hear of His goodness. Even if I never met them or knew how He did it, knowing that He would bring me joy. So much joy. That was enough for me.

Purpose in our pain makes it so much more bearable. God always has reasons for the things He does and the things He allows. He didn't cause my ski accident to punish me or make my life miserable, but He could use it to help me grow in my understanding of who He is and how deeply He loves me. And He could use it to bless others. My therapist was spot-on. Clearly, there was much I needed to learn about applying Romans 8:28 to my own life.

God was helping me find joy by having me focus on His purpose in the pain—a real-life opportunity to learn to keep my eyes on the prize—but there was still some lingering fear that I would always have a head injury. To release the fear completely, I knew I had to submit my life to Him. This meant asking Him to be in control. My Bible dictionary says submission is "voluntary yielding to another." Submission is letting go completely, no matter what. It's like releasing the handlebars on a full-speed motorcycle and trusting I won't crash.

Occasionally I used to ride my mountain bike to the church where I served on staff as the youth director. In a chat with the pastor just before riding home, I learned his sister could also ride no handed. He couldn't do it as a child or adult and was surprised I still could. He wondered how far I could ride without touching, but I had no clue. That day, I was curious enough to learn the answer: seven miles. Was it stupid to ride seven miles no handed? Yes. Was it fun? Yes! (It was less stupid than the time I Snapchatted Robbie from my bike. That night, I got to cohost the graduation baccalaureate service with gashes on my elbows and knees).

If I wanted to stop being afraid, I had to let go of the handlebars and let God steer my bike. This meant trusting that if the Lord wanted me to stay like this for the rest of my earthly days, He knew what He was doing. There would be a purpose. He would use it for good, and I could trust Him, bottom line.

The time had come to kick fear to the curb and let faith rule. I clung to the truth of Romans 8:28 one night as I lay in bed, Rick sleeping peacefully beside me. With grateful tears of faith—and, finally, not fear—streaming onto my pillow, I let go of trying to control my life. I let go of thinking I was responsible for my healing. Instead, I placed my healing, wholeness, family, business, and everything I loved in the hands of a God who loves me. I trusted that despite my circumstances, God is who He says He is: loving, merciful, and good.

Life was still messy, but it brought me so much joy to let go and crash into His arms. God caught me, and I felt safe. No matter what, I was His. It brought me comfort to know that even if the symptoms never resolved on this side of heaven, God would use it all for joy somehow. That night, I slept deeply.

"You make known to me the path of life; you will fill me with joy in your presence, with eternal pleasures at your right hand."
(Psalm 16:11)

Thankfully, this is when my story began to change.

Messy Joy Spill-Your-Guts Journal Questions:

1. How do you hope to act in a crisis situation? What are you actually like? Give examples and share your thoughts.
2. Whom can you share your feelings and be 100 percent transparent with?
3. In your own life, when did you experience a great difficulty and need to trust in God's timing? What did you learn?
4. Looking back, when do you wish you had trusted in God's timing sooner? What was the outcome?
5. If God chose to wait until heaven to heal you from your deepest hurt, what might you have the opportunity to learn?
6. Share a time when you felt confident that God was fighting your battle for you.
7. Has your life changed in an instant? What did you learn about the Lord? About yourself?
8. What are your greatest fears? Have you submitted them to God in prayer?
9. Has Satan used fear to pull you away from God and rob you of joy? What other tools does he use in your life?
10. What are your honest thoughts about seeing a counselor and/or life coach?
11. Write about a time you felt especially stuck. What helped you to move forward?

12. Is there something you are stuck in right now? What is it? How does it compare to the power of the Lord?

13. Do you believe you can have joy even if your circumstances never change? If yes, how? If not, why?

14. Is your faith on your Joy Bucket List? Why or why not?

15. Let's apply Romans 8:28 to your life. What might be some purpose in pain you have experienced or are experiencing now? What good did/might God bring from it?

16. Have you asked God to use all things in your life for good? Are there any in particular that you would find relief in submitting to Him?

17. If someone were to listen to Paul Harvey share about you on *The Rest of the Story*, how would you like for it to end? What steps can you take today to move in that direction?

18. Are you able to let go of knowing how things are going to work out? Do you need to have the answers? What might this say about you?

19. My story about the ocean bringing me joy brings up these questions: What brings you joy in nature? Are these on your joy bucket list?

20. What are the greatest parts of your life that you have submitted to the Lord? Elaborate on your experience of letting go and trusting fully in the Lord with the things that mean the most to you. What did God teach you?

21. Do you believe God is who He says He is? What effect does this have on the amount of joy in your life?

CHAPTER 7

Why Does God Keep Wanting Me to Learn the Same Lessons?

Yes, this is the point where my story improved. You might be wondering, was it because I submitted my life to God? Was that some kind of magical formula? I'll never know. What I do know is, God doesn't work like some wish-granting genie who is waiting for us to utter the perfect combination of words. He isn't Santa Claus, even though many of us have been guilty of praying some version of *Dear God, Please bring me the tooth fairy for Christmas. Amen.*

God knows all that we hold in our hearts and has great plans for us anyway. He knew the depth of my sincerity—He saw my hands come off the handlebars and reach for Him that night—and He is good. I'll focus on that because it's what I know for sure.

God had been orchestrating some details for my good, and it seemed the time had come to make them known. On day 75 of my recovery journey, new components entered my story, and they gave me new hope. There were three things in particular: 1) A close friend saw an ad on social media for a training on concussion recovery and sent it to me. 2) My concussion specialist referred me to physical therapy for my neck.

And 3) as scared as I am of needles, I listened to my integrative medicine doctor and made an acupuncture appointment.

It was a big day. Little did I know, God was going to use it to help me learn an important lesson once and for all. The one about the goodness in asking for help.

Lessons are funny. One thing I distinctly remember my mom saying as I grew up—because my "exuberance for life" meant she said it more than once—"Robin, you can't learn anything the first time. It takes you three times to learn your lesson."

Heck, she probably had to say that three times.

Did anyone ever say this about you? Is there any truth to it?

I am laughing as I type this because the truth is, my mom was way off: it often took me more than three times to learn some lessons.

> *Ladies and gentlemen, the points have been added up,*
> *and the final score is . . .*
> *The Lesson ("It is good to ask for help."): 283*
> *The Student (Robin asking for help): 6*

In all seriousness, isn't it a relief that God doesn't keep score for any of us? Not only does He keep giving us opportunities to learn the things that can really bless us, but out of His crazy love, He opts out of remembering our mistakes.

"It [love] does not dishonor others, it is not self-seeking, it is not easily angered, it keeps no record of wrongs."
(1 Corinthians 13:5)

Evidently, the Big Guy really wants to bless me with the ability to ask for help because opportunities have been plentiful.

While I was impatiently waiting for my life to return, I had opportunities on the daily. It's no surprise: I failed, and I paid the price.

I failed again and again to ask for help, and over and over I paid the price. It was a cycle of wash, rinse, and repeat that went on far longer than three times.

I felt very much like Paul, wondering why he couldn't break the cycle of sin. Tell me I'm not the only one who can relate to this:

**"I do not understand what I do. For what I want to do I do not do,
but what I hate I do. And if I do what I do not want to do,
I agree that the law is good. As it is, it is no longer I myself who do
it, but it is sin living in me. For I know that good itself does not
dwell in me, that is, in my sinful nature. For I have the desire to do
what is good, but I cannot carry it out. For I do not do the good I
want to do, but the evil I do not want to do—this I keep on doing.
Now if I do what I do not want to do, it is no longer
I who do it, but it is sin living in me that does it."**
(Romans 7:15–20)

I'm no Paul, but if I wrote that, it would read, "I want to do what's right, but I'm a sinful screw up and I need help."

I had given God control of my messy life and been rewarded with immeasurable joy. However, I still refused to allow people to help me on a regular basis. He had plans to teach me that asking for help was going to be critical to moving on with my life. I could not do this on my own. There were small examples of this truth and one really big one.

As one small example, I remember how Rick's birthday could have ended in disaster. As it approached in the spring, I had a great conversation with Missy about all the fun things we could do to celebrate him. We wanted him to feel loved on his birthday, so we thought about what gift would speak to him most. After a long, cold winter, we settled on surprising him with a family day of kayaking together. We had never gone, and he is such a lover of the outdoors and family time, it seemed like the perfect combination. Robbie came home from college, and the three of us were so excited when we kidnapped him on a warm spring day and took off for the livery.

The thing I hadn't considered was how hard it would be to think through the countless steps required to maneuver a kayak down a river with a lingering concussion. The plan seemed innocent enough to me, but I was wrong. All the backpaddling required to steer, remembering to paddle on the left to turn right, and avoiding limbs and rocks caught up to me. Within the first thirty minutes, I was fighting back tears, feeling so stupid for not being able to steer my kayak without freaking out. Coming close to so many boulders was really scary. It wasn't white water rafting on the Colorado River; it was a relaxing family day on a small current going through a quiet neighborhood, but we still had hours to go, and my head felt like it was going to explode. It was harder than I had expected to stay calm enough to think clearly. I didn't want to feel helpless and emotional and ruin Rick's birthday, so all I could do was ask for help.

It turned out to be such a great move—and a real blessing. Of course, Rick was glad to help. We beached our kayaks and Rick tied the front of mine to the back of his. The next thing we knew, we were like a floating train. I was riding in style, being towed in the glorious sun by the birthday boy.

Yes, there was something wrong with this picture,
but I didn't have to think, and I wasn't complaining.

It was great being close enough to talk about the green leaves popping out, laugh about the way the kids raced ahead and thought a muskrat was a beaver, and share the experience. I paddled behind him, fear gone, having fun. Asking for help meant I felt safe and was able to pour love and kindness into my husband on his birthday.

This is just one example of how my family helped me, as they were there for me constantly. They were my rock. Everyone should be so blessed.

A second memory comes up of a time I refused to ask them and it ended a lot differently. Robbie was at college, and Rick and Missy were at the dining room table. I was nearby, assembling a mailing to the neighbors. We have a neighborhood association, and I am proud to say that early in my injury, I did ask for someone else to take my role of secretary.

Maybe I should add a point to the tally above.

Rick would have done it, of course, but he was already serving as president. In the end, no one took the role. It forced me into trying to keep up with group correspondence. Thankfully, Rick filled in from time to time, but it bothered me that he had to do extra work, and I was determined to type the minutes and send them out after one meeting in particular.

While organizing things brought me joy before I hit my head, after, I really struggled. It was so hard to make the basic, logical decisions needed for things to flow. I had papers and envelopes in a state of disarray all over the counter as I attempted to stuff and address the envelopes. I kept losing my spot and screwing up the handwritten addresses. It was so frustrating. The messy counter was a reflection of the chaos in my mind. I tried methodically to get the job done, but I had to keep stopping to fix my mistakes.

The looks on the faces of Rick and Missy as I grunted, exhaled, and later cried in frustration were so sad. They wanted to set me free from the trap of being in my head. It would have taken them a few minutes tops. They offered.

I refused and kept trying to address and stuff the mailing, getting angrier at myself by the minute. Finally, I walked out to the mailbox and shoved the envelopes inside. Admittedly, I used more force than was needed to close the door. I could have thrown those meeting minutes to their final destinations; I was so upset. Storming inside the house, the only thing I wanted was to lie down alone and cry. The next thing I knew, I was isolated, broken . . . over mail.

I could have known the joy of receiving help had I asked for it, but instead I believed the lies of the enemy of my soul. My reward for self-sufficiency: misery.

Satan: 284

Robin: 6

You are right again, God . . . I still need to work on this.

Thankfully, God gave me the strength to ask for a lot of professional help. I don't know where I would be without my counselor, physical therapist, concussion course instructors, concussion specialist, acupuncturist, integrative medicine doctor, and family doctor.

The help I received through the Concussion Fix course was like water to my desert-hardened outlook. I believe this course turned things around for me. It was online, and I jumped at it. Because the doctor knew so much about healing head injuries, I hung on every word. I remember feeling like he was an angel based on the way he spoke about my crazy symptoms like he knew my story, but he was a chiropractor who had treated over a thousand head injuries. He really got my attention when he said that conventional medicine often misses the boat by prescribing the "wait and see" approach, when a more aggressive approach is often more helpful. He offered a video-based course with weekly live Q-and-As. He shared some awesome testimonials of helping people heal who had far worse injuries than mine.

I devoured the videos and found so much comfort in getting my questions answered. I learned I wasn't alone as I shared openly with other students at the live Q-and-As. It was a neat club of injured adventure seekers just trying to think straight. Above all else, I made huge progress when I realized that one of the five components of treatment was getting permission to return to life without fearing my actions would make my head permanently worse. Previously, I'd felt like a guilty caged animal who was wrong to try anything. I was dying to live fully again and do it without shame. It was somewhat frightening to try new things after months of being told that rest was the solution. Suddenly, an expert in concussions gave me permission to go for walks, get together with people, and work without fear that it would permanently mess up my head. I learned it would hurt, but it would heal, and repeating the cycle would only make things better. It was like being let out of prison.

As the fear disappeared and the joy of living began to return, the concussion cloud lifted a little more each day. I began to feel human again, and it felt incredible. I would highly recommend Concussion Fix to anyone with a concussion, no matter how long ago it happened. You can always search for it online, or contact me on my website (joytotheworldcoaching.com) for a link to get 10 percent off. This course made such a difference for me, and I can only pray others will find as much relief from it.

But it was time to add physical therapy per the course and my concussion specialist. I also wanted to add in acupuncture as suggested by my integrative medicine doctor. As much as I hated to add to anyone else's to-do lists, the point came when asking for help became essential, because I still could not drive.

Not being able to drive was one of the hardest parts of having a head injury. I love to be free to choose what I do and when. This is a big part of why I love biking so much, because it brings me joy to decide spontaneously where to go and which mud puddles to aim for. Not being able to drive left me feeling like the rest of the world was moving forward, while I was just sitting there, waiting to get better.

I did try driving a few times in the early months, and even now the memory of it makes me shake my head. It was so different than I thought it would be. Driving was complicated; it made my head want to explode. The number of safety-related decisions that my brain had to make in any given moment was staggering, and it left me feeling spaced out, exhausted, and honestly scared for the well-being of the other people on the road. Having recently read Dale Earnhardt Jr.'s tales of driving a racecar with several concussions in *Racing to the Finish*, I wonder how driving was possible for him at all, let alone racing. My story was so different, but all head injuries are, in fact, very different. After a few scary fifteen-minute attempts at driving, I quit trying.

So I needed help to get to my first acupuncture appointment. It was almost eleven weeks after my accident, and we had just celebrated Easter. I remember trying to smile at my sister-in-law's house on Easter, so thankful to get out of the house and be together but struggling so hard with the activity and noise. It was a beautiful, sunny day, and the party was outside because of COVID. My mind was racing trying to keep up with the conversation, and even though it was good for me, all I could think about was curling up in fetal position in a dark room. Even in the great expanse of outdoor space, warm sun, and fresh air, I felt overwhelmed by the mental chaos from trying to engage in hours of conversation, and I asked to go home early. It was so disappointing.

Hopefully acupuncture would help, and social gatherings would be possible again. Since I felt really safe with my sister, I asked her to take me. Tracy was off work for spring break, and I only had to ask for one ride. God's timing was perfect. She called me frequently to check on me, her worried tone always evident, and she didn't hesitate when I asked for help.

Think what you will, but I have to tell you that I have a huge fear of needles. I've passed out many times getting shots and having blood drawn. Acupuncture was never on my list of things to try. I was scared to death. But I was desperate. Paying out of pocket to get poked had to be proof that I was willing to try anything to get back to normal.

The appointment felt really weird because it was all so new and I was filled with fear. The doctor, a seventh-generation acupuncturist from China, asked a host of questions before inserting a bunch of tiny needles in my back, neck, and head. Thankfully, they didn't cause pain and I didn't lose consciousness. I had to lie still for an hour, facedown on a massage table. Facing my fear led to a huge emotional release, and I cried the whole time, tears dripping onto the floor, runny nose filling up my face mask. I couldn't move and wipe them away. Thankfully, my hair hung down and the doctor couldn't see what a mess I was when she came in to turn and flick the needles.

I had planned to go once and celebrate by eating dinner on fancy dishes that night. However, there was something comforting about the doctor. I trusted her. After the appointment, I felt like I was floating in space as I agreed to buy a package. I had to wonder what she thought as I struggled to fill out my check. Concentrating on what to write on each line was plenty for my brain that day. Tracy, as concerned and helpful as she possibly could have been, drove me home in a quiet, peaceful car. I could hardly wait to sleep in my bed. I slept for hours that day.

Thanks be to God, that was a day filled with wins! I asked for help, accepted it, and faced a major fear, which had potential to help my brain heal. But there was more. In allowing my sister to drive me, I allowed her to love me in a tangible way. She had been worrying and watching for months, and suddenly she was able to do something concrete. I didn't see it at the time, but allowing her to help took a major load off her mind. My fear of adding to her burden was unfounded, and in the end, letting her help actually lightened her emotional load. Who knew?

This was a lesson that was good to learn.

Why does God want us to keep learning the same lessons? Because He is good. He loves us relentlessly.

"The Lord appeared to us in the past, saying: 'I have loved you with an everlasting love; I have drawn you with unfailing kindness.'"

(Jeremiah 31:3)

I love that so much. An everlasting love. Unfailing kindness.

Whether we need to learn to ask for help, or quit a bad habit, or make Him our top priority, He is not going to give up. He will bless us and help us learn what He needs for us to know. Even when we are too stupid to see blessings for what they are, He gives them to us, again and again. Some of our greatest lessons can be our greatest blessings. Learning to ask for help has been just that for me.

Thank You, God. You really know how to love.

But He wasn't done loving me. I needed to keep learning this one. Since work was starting for Tracy, I had to find another way to get to the appointments in my package. Plus, I was ready to add physical therapy in another city on my acupuncture days. Acupuncture was an hour in one direction, and PT was twenty minutes on the opposite side of home. Rick and the kids weren't around, or they would have jumped at the chance to help. I hated to think of asking someone to give up so much time, but I knew I needed to get to these appointments. It was time to get over my fear of asking for help. I thought of someone who was always checking in on me, worried, wanting to help.

My mom.

What you don't know is this was a big ask, because my mom and I weren't in the greatest place.

But before that will make sense, I need to share some stories with you. These are stories I have kept quiet for years—one I have repressed for the better part of my life. Because they tie in, and because God is making it clear the time has come to share more about how He loves us and brings us joy through our worst nightmares, they need to be told now.

Messy Joy Spill-Your-Guts Journal Questions:

1. Can you think of a time you learned a lesson right away? Why might this be?

2. Think of something God has forgiven you for. Thank Him for not keeping score.

3. Have you ever felt like Paul in Romans 7, struggling to break free from a bad habit? How did your faith help? What specific advice might you have for your younger self?

4. What lesson are you walking through over and over? What are your thoughts about learning this particular lesson? What might God want from you? For you?

5. Can you think of a time you asked for and received genuine help? Describe the situation and how it made you feel.

6. Can you think of a time you were too stubborn to learn a lesson, like my story of completing the mailing myself rather than asking for help? How did things end up for you? What impact did this have on your level of joy? On your relationship with God?

7. If you struggle to ask for help, do you prefer to ask professionals or friends and family? Why? What might this say about you?

8. When you read my story of facing my fear of needles, did it remind you of a fear you've faced and overcome? What impact

did overcoming this fear have on your life? How did it affect your understanding of God?

9. Is there a fear the Lord is ready to help you face right now?

10. In your own words, why does God want you to keep learning the same lessons?

CHAPTER 8

Can I Just Fix This with Mac and Cheese?

So, yes, there's a story that needs to be told about finding joy in my relationship with my mom, but before that can make sense, you need to know about some other things that threatened to rob me of the remaining joy I had. It seemed life was about to get messier.

I will start by making a confession.

It's a good thing I haven't practiced as a nutritionist in a while, because they'd probably pull my license after reading what I am about to say.

Here we go. Ahem.

My name is Robin Shear and I love Kraft Mac and Cheese. It's one of my favorite foods of all time. I have probably eaten hundreds of boxes. I know I have a problem. I never thought I could live without it

Whew. I feel better.

This ties in to the messy joy thing, I promise.

So, two months before my ski accident, my functional medicine doctor ran tests because I was tired so often and had been experiencing so many headaches. In the process, she found that I had *Candida* overgrowth in my gut. Apparently, *Candida* is a fungus that everyone has, but it doesn't fall into the "if a little bit is good, a lot is better" category. While I didn't think I had many symptoms from it, I had too much in my system, and we needed to get it into the normal range.

No big deal.

It turns out a lot of things can make *Candida* grow, including stress and a diet filled with sugar and refined carbs.

Uh oh.

Back in my past life as a dietitian, you can bet that my nutritional intake was pretty clean. Eating well makes you feel better, perform at your best, and live longer. But when I dove into the world of youth ministry, things got a little junkier. It's no secret that teens like nachos and brownies. Teens and their youth leaders.

Not only that, but the stress of trying to get my joy coaching business off the ground meant an increased amount of emotional eating . . . and I wasn't reaching for spinach. It was so much easier to grab a handful of something salty or sweet than to make yet another decision. Starting a business was H-A-R-D and my number one cure for the hardest days was mac and cheese, nature's "perfect food."

And wouldn't you know, working from home meant very close proximity to the kitchen.

Heaven help me.

So my doctor ran tests and found the *Candida*. She planned to work on some other issues I was having first, then address the *Candida* about a month later. But then Christmas came, and we were recovering from COVID. My doctor warned me that we needed to wait.

Evidently the treatment was mentally taxing, and she wanted me to be strong before beginning the protocol.

My ski accident was near the end of January. You could say I was already mentally taxed.

But I was also determined to prove how strong I was.

By early February I was going stir-crazy, wanting to fix something, anything. So I started doing little bits of *Candida* research on my own. I found that diet played a big part, and the short-term *Candida* cleanse diet treatment plan was very low carb and eliminated several foods:

- yeast products (all bread products and crackers)
- pasta
- starchy vegetables
- sugar, corn syrup, honey, natural sweeteners
- high fructose fruits
- alcohol
- white carbs
- milk and cheese
- a long list of condiments like vinegar, ketchup, mustard, salad dressing, and mayo
- caffeine
- processed meats
- trans fats
- peanut butter

Which meant eliminating all joy.

So, no mac and cheese. No PB and J with my mac and cheese. And definitely no wine with my PB and J and mac and cheese.

Until the *Candida* cleared up, I was pretty much left with two choices:

- vegetables
- protein

You can imagine my excitement.

However, I wanted to get the excess *Candida* out of my system as soon as possible—probably a control thing, since my head pain was so out of my control—so in early February I just started finding substitutes. And eliminating stuff. And adding a whole lot of vegetables.

It kind of woke up the sleeping dietitian inside of me. It was a challenge, and I accepted it readily, most of the time.

But man, it was hard, and that mac and cheese shelf was still full, the boxes staring at me, promising they could make me feel better about everything.

I had to learn other ways to cope with the bad days. Food would no longer be my solution because stress-eating eggs didn't really appeal to me.

God is just good like that, isn't He? He sees what we have begun to rely on, in some cases even idolize, and He gently reminds us that He is better. So, time with Him became my go-to. I leaned heavily on prayer and as much Christian music as my head could take. I stuck with it for the first month.

My birthday was in March, and I combined all kinds of online food hacks so I could still enjoy birthday cake for breakfast. This is a huge tradition in our house. We love birthdays in our family, following the pattern of how my mom made our birthdays feel like holidays from the minute we woke up. The only difference: at the Shear house, birthdays always start with cake for breakfast.

Why? I really wanted cake for breakfast as a kid. My mom's answer was the classic parent reply, "When you are an adult, you can do things your way." So, the first year we were married, we had cake for breakfast, and we called my mom while we ate it.

Fast-forward: Our kids are the ages we were as newlyweds. Out of all the things we have done as parents, having cake for breakfast is the first one that comes up when they say what traditions they're going to carry on. Who knew it could be so simple?

For three months straight, I prayed more than I have in my life and ate squeaky clean, following the list to the letter. I tried hard to obey Scripture:

"Be joyful in hope, patient in affliction, faithful in prayer."
(Romans 12:12)

And then in May, I asked my doctor if I could begin the full *Candida* cleanse treatment plan.

Yes, I knew that adding the cleanse's medications would be mentally taxing, and I was still dealing with my concussion.

And I had just stopped taking an antidepressant cold turkey (with permission of my specialist) because it didn't help the head pain and the side effects were horrendous.

And I had just had my first COVID shot.

Who knew it would be the perfect storm?

My doctor put together a regimen of special meds and supplements for me to take five times a day for the next thirty days, and I began the official *Candida* cleanse.

I was so glad to get going and move on. I had been planning a Myrtle Beach family vacation to surprise Robbie on his twenty-first birthday, set for June 2. I didn't want anything to get in the way of our fun. We needed this. After months of feeling like a prisoner, *I* needed this.

Clarity of thought in planning a surprise of this magnitude would be challenging on a good brain, let alone one with a concussion and hardly any carbs for brain fuel. In order to pull off a surprise, details are everything.

I distinctly remember the day I was buying the airline tickets, after secretly talking to Robbie's boss to arrange work off without his knowledge. I was home alone, hands shaking, so excited I couldn't think straight. I sat on the couch, typing everyone's legal names into the ticket order form. And that's when I saw it. In order to board the plane, the plane tickets had to match their driver's licenses exactly.

And . . . for the life of me, I felt like my brain kept timing out as I questioned what my family's middle names were.

I am the kind of person who can rattle off all kinds of memories and dates, and here I was, unsure of my favorite people's middle names. I could have gotten up and checked their passports for assurance. But I was too stubborn and prideful. I felt like it was stuff I should know. So I wrestled with my inner demons and filled the form out, hoping it was right, wondering, mad at myself for having to wonder. My heart was pounding as I submitted the online order. I prayed the names were right, knowing that if I messed them up, the tickets couldn't be changed.

You can imagine my relief when I learned that everything was okay.

Stupid, I know. I earned it. Call me Rose. The scene where Rose clings to the Titanic wreckage in the freezing water and tells Jack, "I'll never let go," is a great depiction of me talking to my pride.

The first night of the official *Candida* cleanse, I did not sleep. At all. My mind was spinning in full force, thoughts flying faster than I could process them. And song lyrics. So many Christian songs were on repeat in my head. It was wild. I tried several relaxation techniques. Deep-breathing patterns. Relaxing one muscle at a time from head to toe. Praying for everyone under the sun. Imagining my body sinking into my mattress. Nothing worked. I felt that God was speaking to me all night long and did not want me to sleep, though admittedly I kept trying. By morning I was exhausted.

And that's when the weird thoughts began.

It's hard for me to describe what thoughts I was having. But I did not feel like myself, and I did not feel in control of my mind. It was racing all over the place, and I felt unsafe. Songs kept coming to mind like downloads from God. One song after another. A playlist was forming that I had nothing to do with. When I recognized that, I solidified it on Spotify and kept it on repeat all day long. By the end of the next day, I was scared of my irrational thoughts and named the playlist "Robin

Brain Songs: God Wins" to remind myself that the weird feeling I had wouldn't last forever.

I'm going to share my playlist with you, because even though it's very personal and might not make a lot of sense, the songs have the potential to help you face whatever you're facing. Music has such power. If you have a Spotify account, just search for this playlist by name.

On that day, I couldn't focus on basic tasks and felt like my eyes were open extra wide, scanning for unseen, unnamed dangers around me. By afternoon I resorted to doing things that were familiar because nothing felt normal, and I desperately needed some familiarity. I put in the movie version of my favorite book (*Same Kind of Different As Me*—promise me you'll read it) but kept getting stressed out, wondering where the plot was going, even though I knew it like the back of my hand. It was too much. I turned it off. I needed something safe, something familiar, something simple. I printed out a connect-the-dots image, slowly concentrating on drawing a line to the next number, trying to restore my mental balance. I was in my late forties struggling to complete a dot-to-dot. It was that bad.

My medication schedule was demanding, and all day I was so afraid that I'd miss one of my five doses and mess everything up. The fear grew throughout the day. It wasn't like me to be so obsessed with getting it right. I put so much pressure on myself to remember to take everything on time and get rid of the extra *Candida*. The medication schedule check sheet I wrote out for guidance and mental relief didn't help me feel organized like I thought it would.

I felt agitated, under pressure, foreign in my mind and body, and scared of harm that I couldn't identify. I remember being outside with the dog in the evening, hoping the fresh air would help. As I walked around the yard with Molly, I was unable to calm down, fearing some kind of danger, feeling like nothing was familiar. I felt as close to psychotic as I've ever been. All of the random flying thoughts made me wonder if this is what people with schizophrenia experience. I came inside and told Rick that I shouldn't be alone the next day.

Was I suicidal? Yes, I think so. I don't understand why. I cannot remember with clarity what I was thinking, but all I knew was, I was scared to be alone and wondering if I was safe.

I started sending SOS voice messages to some of my safest, closest friends. I wish I knew what I'd sent, but phones often automatically delete voice messages after a while. I just remember feeling like I needed to share from a place of honesty and let someone else know about the chaos that was brewing in my mind. If you got a weird message, you know who you are!

The interesting thing was how God gave me peace at night. All night. For a second night in a row, I did not sleep a minute. I felt like I was on the receiving end of some very direct messages from God, much like the night before. While my mind was too chaotic in the daytime to remember what God had shared at night, I was so relieved when He showed up again instead of allowing me to sleep. This time I was ready. I wanted to remember what He said when daylight—and what seemed like all hell—broke loose in my mind. So on that second night, I typed highlights of our time together in my notes app.

I don't expect this to make a lot of sense to anyone else because at times it was like a conversation with a friend that was flowing all over the place. In general, I was writing to myself, knowing I'd want the help in the morning. And while this conversation is really personal and I could be judged all kinds of ways, I feel strongly that God is telling me to include it here, every single word. God, be glorified in the sharing of this.

WHAT'S TRUE DURING CHAOS
God gave me these truths during the night.
This is temporary.
God is everything.
I do not have to understand anyway.
It's okay.

The battle is the Lord's, so stop trying to fight.

Trust Him.

Peace is the gift God freely gives, so accept it. You want acceptance and so does the Lord.

Peace be with you.

Have peace.

Accept peace.

Breathe in deeply—God.

Exhale deeply—all else.

I do not have to control.

Pressure is used by the enemy and takes me away from focusing on the big truth of God—of God being in control, not me.

Accepting pressure is wrong.

Refusing pressure because He is everything—and God is enough—this is right.

I will not believe the lie that it is up to me.

It is not my decision.

I do not have to understand.

I don't have to get it. Yay!

I can and should let it go.

There is nothing wrong with me.

The self-judgment has got to stop because God wants peace inside.

Accept peace. Breathe it in. Wow, it's right there, a breath away, and you don't have to make it—or force it—to happen. It just is.

Because He is who He says He is.

The great I AM.

HE IS.

HE WILL BE.

I cannot keep a wall around my mind to try to hold it together.

I am afraid of losing control of everything, and the fear is like a wall of Jericho all around my mind, and it has to come down.

Choosing to take one stone from the fear wall is up to me—and when I do that, I am choosing peace—because God has been surrounding me, patiently waiting for me to invite Him in to my control center.

When the enemy gives pressure, I choose peace, and I let go of fear—and God restores and makes all things right.

Behold, I make all things new.

I joyfully and wholeheartedly accept that it's really His control center. Thanks be to God.

He floods in peacefully, and everything is right and new.

I receive wisdom from Him when I ask for it with confidence because this is what He wants to give, and He gives it with joy.

I will count it all joy when I am persecuted for His sake because trials produce patience, and patience is perfect because it brings peace.

It's all pointing to the same message, and there are several ways to get there because they are connected, so pick one and do not worry it's wrong.

Wisdom from God allows me to love the way He loves.

Asking for wisdom isn't only about the mind; it is about the mind and the heart uniting.

Do what You want.

Wisdom from God is what is needed to connect my head and my heart.

I have not understood wisdom and that is okay because I do not have to understand—all I have to do is trust that God is everything. Really everything.

Trust. Believe. Accept. Obey. Love.

The songs that God puts in my head have messages that are intentional, and He will reveal His reason at the perfect time.

Do not try to turn those music lyrics messages off when they seem ill timed or inconvenient.

Seek true peace.

Yes, you have experienced peace, and you will experience that again. Any difficulty is temporary.

You can have help because God wants to help you and that is enough.
You do not have to be afraid.
He will never leave your side.
You don't have to remember; He will be there even when you forget and cannot think clearly.
It is okay. And it is going to be okay.
Unbelievable how You gave me songs in advance during acupuncture for weeks. You were meeting me in acupuncture and preparing me for this battle now. You gave me these truths when I was completely still and entirely focused on You and only You. Truth comes in stillness. Make time for quiet moments because the world is loud and God whispers. God whispers.
Be still and know that I am God.
There is a God, and you are not it.
You should not try to control.
Let go. He is trustworthy.
Do not fear for I am with you. Do not be afraid. I will be with you wherever you go.
The dark is as day to You.
The dark is not to be feared because He is there, and He can see and think clearly.
He can do it and you don't have to.
Oh, my God, You are so good.

You would think that spending two nights wide awake would have left me exhausted, but instead, I was energized. I got to spend a good sixteen hours with God, and my joy was off the charts! I screenshotted these words and saved them in Google photos so I could read them again and again in the days that followed. Sometimes I started my day by meditating on one of these truths that the Lord shared with me. I often opened my phone and revisited His messages of love to me throughout the day. I clung to them—and all the songs God had given me—like someone drifting in the ocean clinging to a ragged life ring. Thankfully, God saw me through the chaos of that perfect storm. It brought entirely new meaning to a story that's told in three of the gospels, as it is told here:

> *That day when evening came, he said to his disciples, "Let us go over to the other side." Leaving the crowd behind, they took him along, just as he was, in the boat. There were also other boats with him. A furious squall came up, and the waves broke over the boat, so that it was nearly swamped. Jesus was in the stern, sleeping on a cushion. The disciples woke him and said to him, "Teacher, don't you care if we drown?"*
>
> *He got up, rebuked the wind and said to the waves, "Quiet! Be still!" Then the wind died down and it was completely calm.*
>
> *He said to his disciples, "Why are you so afraid? Do you still have no faith?"*

**They were terrified and asked each other,
"Who is this? Even the wind and the waves obey him!"**
(Mark 4:35–41)

I knew what it felt like to have an out-of-control storm in my heart, mind, and gut be calmed by a God who is impenetrably in control.

Each day, my mental clarity returned more. Not only that, but two years of monthly debilitating migraines, each of which cost me two days minimum, came to an abrupt end. They were just gone. I don't know how He did it, and I don't have to. He showed me that He is in control and that He is very, very good.

Oh, and we went on that trip to Myrtle Beach! We surprised Robbie good and had a ton of fun doing anything we wanted. But that's another book for another day.

As for the *Candida*? The treatment worked. It's been within normal limits ever since. I can eat anything I want. My diet has remained pretty clean. I hardly think about mac and cheese.

Kraft, you promise a little taste of heaven, and that's cool, but I'm not buying it, because God is the only one who truly delivers.

Messy Joy Spill-Your-Guts Journal Questions:

1. In general, how aligned is your diet with what's best for you?
2. When you are feeling stressed, tired, or overwhelmed, how do you cope? What, if anything, do you turn to or reach for?
3. How important is it to be in control of a situation?
4. Write about a time when you learned it was good to let go of control.
5. What have you begun to rely on, or maybe even idolize, and what's God's view of the situation?
6. Traditions are important. If you are a parent, what traditions have your kids (or will your kids have) carried forward? What traditions have you carried on from your family? How do these traditions make you feel?
7. I shared that I felt I needed to prove I was strong enough to endure the *Candida* cleanse when the timing wasn't best. Can you relate? Write about a time you felt the need to prove something without waiting for the right time. What happened? What did you learn?
8. How do you feel about planning surprises? About being surprised?
9. What songs really speak to you when you are in a time of need? What songs tell the world who you are right now? Who you were in your past?
10. When God wants to speak to you at "inconvenient" times (like at night perhaps), how do you respond? How would you like to

respond? How can you be more open to having conversation with Him when He is calling to you?

11.   Did you download the Spotify playlist? Are there any songs that you needed to hear for your own situation?

12.   When you need to send an SOS message, whom do you send it to? Why?

13.   If you have ever heard directly from God, write about your experience here.

14.   Do any of the messages that God gave me about my situation resonate with you and your situation? Why? Write your thoughts here.

15.   Write about a time when Jesus calmed the storm in your life. How did He show up for you?

16.   How does spending time alone with God make you feel? What effect does it have on the amount of joy in your day?

CHAPTER 9

Why Sleep When You Can Be Having a Prayer Breakthrough?

This might be a quick chapter, but the experience was so significant, I have to include it. Consider this bathroom reading that could help you to have a prayer breakthrough.

It's strange, but when I was lying awake at night during the first two nights of my *Candida* cleanse, one theme that kept coming up over and over was the need to pray for wisdom.

Weird, I know.

I'll be the first to admit that I have never considered myself the wisest person. See the chapter on how it took me three times minimum to learn pretty much anything worthwhile. I often follow my heart, which tends to be spontaneous and impulsive. That's why one of my most requested group talks is "Burnout Buster: The Joy of Being Spontaneous." I don't even offer onc called "The Joy of Wisdom."

If you want a spontaneous, joy-boosting idea that won't cost
you any extra money, go through a drive-through line in reverse.
I guarantee it will make you laugh!
A close second is running outside to jump in puddles
and dance in a rainstorm. You've seen the idea plastered everywhere . . . do

it. You'll feel so alive! Don't worry about your clothes.
I jumped in so many puddles to get the right shot for the cover
of this book, and all of the mud came out.
And anyway, dirty kids are happy kids.

I've never considered spontaneity to be a bad thing, but a little wisdom mixed in could make for a great one-two combo.

But for some reason, perhaps due to the nudging of the Holy Spirit, this whole weird mental *Candida* experience really made me crave wisdom.

The interesting thing was, that first night of sleeplessness, I realized I really didn't know what wisdom was.

Lying there in the dark and hoping not to disturb my sleeping husband, I dimmed my screen and looked it up online. Google defined wisdom as "the quality of having experience, knowledge, and good judgment." Hmm. Sounded kind of boring.

I was curious what the Bible said. One search turned up a plethora of passages on wisdom, including this one:

"But the wisdom that comes from heaven is first of all pure;
then peace-loving, considerate, submissive, full of mercy and good
fruit, impartial and sincere. Peacemakers who sow in peace
reap a harvest of righteousness."
(James 3:17–18)

Reading this passage made fireworks go off in my heart. This sounded amazing!

I am certainly no expert on the subject of wisdom, but one thing's for sure: my understanding of it had been limited my whole life. The irony. Prior to my late-night encounters with the Lord, I had always viewed wisdom as being knowledgeable, having all the answers, or at least understanding the basis for them. But that was only part of it.

As I began to dig into Scripture and pray for God to help me understand what wisdom was, something became very clear to me. Having wisdom didn't just mean having all the answers. It meant understanding God's ways *so that I could love better.*

Knowledge plus love: talk about a one-two combo.

It was more than just knowing right from wrong. Wisdom was knowing more of the heart and mind of God so that I could not only think more like Him but also love more like Him.

My prayer became, *Dude, sign me up for wisdom!*

This was finally something I could get excited about. For the first time in my life, that night I earnestly prayed for wisdom, not because I thought I needed it but because I wanted it.

It was so cool how God met me where I was. He allowed for a couple of Bible verses I had meditated on previously to come to mind:

"This is the confidence we have in approaching God: that if we ask anything according to his will, he hears us. And if we know that he hears us—whatever we ask—we know that we have what we asked of him."
(1 John 5:14–15)

The more I contemplated this verse, the more excited I got. I began to realize that the other times I had prayed for wisdom, I did so with uncertainty. Like, *God, please give me wisdom, if you think I can handle it.* There was no confidence in my prayer. I was already giving God an out. It's no wonder He didn't dump wisdom into me then.

This time, because of this verse in particular, I knew that I could pray with confidence, because *of course* thinking and loving like God were in line with His will. Why wouldn't He want me to have that? Why wouldn't He want you to have it too?

Even if the thing that you seek isn't necessarily wisdom (although it's pretty sweet—you should go for it!), some questions to ask yourself are

- Is the thing that I seek in alignment with His will?
- Am I praying for it with confidence or trepidation?
- Essentially, do I believe God will grant this to me?
- And, of course, will it bring joy?

This one was shared earlier, but the other passage that kept repeating in my heart was, "God is not the author of confusion, but of peace" (1 Corinthians 14:33 KJV).

Let me tell you, peace was starting to sound really, really good. This was when my mental confusion was really picking up from the *Candida* cleanse and I began to question if I would ever know sanity again. You know how it is when you are in the thick of things:

- It's all you know. That's it.
- There is no end in sight, and you are left with more questions than answers.
- Later you have the whole story and can see from a different perspective, but in the moment you only know what you know.

That's what it was like for me, wondering if I'd ever feel peace again. I am an optimist, but this crazy-train brain was downright scary.

Parents, I have to interject here on behalf of kids.
In all my years of working with kids in youth ministry,
this is one thing that kept coming up over and over.
Kids wish parents could remember what it was like to be a kid.
This type of tunnel-vision thinking is very much how kids see their
problems, and they often feel criticized for it. The thing is,
the moment they are in is all they know for sure. If you're a parent, let me
encourage you to remember what that felt like to be an uncertain young
person. Allow yourself to feel the fear again, because having empathy will
allow you to be present for your kids when they are stuck and spinning.

Your focused presence means everything. They need you.
And now, back to our regularly scheduled broadcast.

So here I am, starting to flip out mentally, not sure if it was going to be my new normal but gently being reminded by a God who loves me that confusion was not His plan. In fact, wisdom was. Wow did this bring me comfort.

I remember a distinct moment from that night of prayer where I felt like I really knew what wisdom was—I wanted to see things from God's eyes and love the way He does—and I believed that I could pray for it with confidence, trusting that He wanted me to have peace. I believed, as this verse from my Grandma Leslie's favorite Bible passage says, that He knew my thoughts, the actual contents of my heart.

"You know when I sit and when I rise;
you perceive my thoughts from afar."
(Psalm 139: 2)

It wasn't like a lightbulb moment; it was more of a heart-download moment. I remember feeling like God was a magnet and I was metal, and when I was drawn to Him and finally made contact, we were inseparably connected, and the dumping of God's heart and mind into mine could begin.

It was the coolest thing.

From a "feel good" perspective, my joy was off the charts. Ever since, I feel like I have this great desire to see things from the Lord's viewpoint so I can love with His love. While I have long prayed for the things that break God's heart to break mine (thank you, Casting Crowns, for singing about this in "Jesus, Friend of Sinners"), this was a new and enhanced version. Now, to whatever extent He would allow, I would be able to understand things and act from a place of love.

I don't know about you, but I am ready to get out of the bathroom and thank God for wisdom.

And since this was a quickie, it's time for a bigger share . . . more proof that when life's not perfect, joy can be found in pain. It's the one mentioned at the very beginning, about making twenty-five attempts to resolve a joy-sucking problem that I had hidden from the world for years. And this one involves you. Let's talk about how you can choose joy when life's messy.

Messy Joy Spill-Your-Guts Journal Questions:

1. Do you ever have sleepless nights? How do you use them for good?
2. What is your understanding of wisdom as God sees it?
3. Are you as wise as you'd like to be?
4. Are there any characteristics of wisdom from the James 3 passage that you long for in particular?
5. How is your prayer life?
6. What difference does your prayer life make in your joy level?
7. Is prayer on your Joy Bucket List?
8. On a scale of one to ten, how confident are you when you approach God in prayer? What would make you more confident?
9. How do you honestly feel about praying for God's will? Is there anything holding you back?
10. Do you believe God will grant you the things that you pray for? Explain.
11. On a scale of one to ten, how's the peace level of your life? What difference would having more peace make on the level of joy you experience on a regular basis? Is there anything you can do about it?
12. Can you think of a time in your life when you were gripped by fear in the moment, but later really understood "hindsight is twenty-twenty"? What advice would you have for yourself the next time you are in a crisis situation?

13. Looking back to when you were younger and couldn't see beyond the moment, who was there for you? What qualities did this person possess? What difference did this person's presence make? Have you ever told this person about the impact they had on you?

14. Can you describe a time when you felt inseparably connected with the heart of God? What was it like? What did it do to the level of joy in your life?

CHAPTER 10

How Do I Choose Joy When the Pain Won't End?

D o you love a good poop story? While it will seem random (and make my kids want to hide under their beds), I need to tell you one.

Have you ever had a "treatable condition" or "resolvable issue" that lasted for so long it sucked the joy right out of you? Something that other people got rid of pretty quickly, but for some reason it stuck around a whole lot longer for you? You tried and tried to shake it, did all kinds of stuff, got worn out from all the trying . . . and then thought about throwing in the towel?

Yeah, me too.

I didn't share it outside my inner circle at the time, but I suffered silently with debilitating foot pain for three years.

Sorry to disappoint you, but that's not the poop part.
You weirdo.

On the outside you wouldn't have known it, as I was determined to live life fully and be of service to other people despite the pain, but there were nights my feet hurt so bad, I crawled to bed.

It started innocently enough. At the time, we had an adorable Brittany Spaniel named Liza Jane. Liza loved to take walks and so did I. She was a great energy match for me. It seemed no matter how far I walked her, as we made the last turn toward home, she always pulled the other way, wanting more. So, our walks got longer. And longer.

Eventually we settled into several routes that ranged from five to ten miles. They were hilly, around lakes and neighborhoods, and we loved tackling them together. (Fun fact: Liza loved plowing through puddles right where this book's cover photo was taken.) The first time Liza ever seemed tired after a walk was when we walked thirteen miles. I was wiped, believe me, and amazingly, she finally was too. We had found the sweet spot.

I never kept great track, but in Liza's lifetime, on the low side, we walked over seven thousand miles. Walking brought so much joy to us both, we headed out several times a week for twelve years. She even went for walks with me after she went blind. The poor little thing had to trust that I wouldn't let her run into stuff and rely on her sense of smell and hearing. Even then, walking seemed to bring her joy . . . which filled my joy bucket too.

> *Hint: is movement on your Joy Bucket List? Get specific.*
> *Which types of movement are the most fun? What about time*
> *with animals? Which kinds make you feel the best?*

Liza was a sweet but mischievous girl who used to eat all kinds of things that she shouldn't have, like acorns off the ground as well as entire containers of Vaseline (including the tubs), a cell phone battery, a bunch of "indestructible" dog toys, a whole rabbit's head, and a bullet.

> *Good times at the Shear house.*

Since they were natural, we didn't think much of her eating acorns until one time, she got so sick, she had to have emergency surgery. The vet had to clear a blockage from all the nuts and sharp fragments of shells in her digestive tract. It was painful for her and expensive for us.

I'd like to say recovering from that one operation taught Liza her lesson.

"I'll never do that again," said no dog ever.

But she ate acorns again and again, like a shop vac with a wiggly stump of a tail. We put a muzzle on her out in the yard. She still found a way.

One time, she greeted my friend Rachel at the driveway with a bloody squirrel hanging out of her muzzle. That was neat. It was Rachel's first time at our house.

So glad you came back, Rach!

As Liza kept getting blocked, we kept trying different things. We couldn't keep paying for the surgery and didn't want to put her through it, so in desperation we had to go old-school: mineral oil and really long walks.

We have so many memories of walking our bloated, farting dog and then cheering when she pooped. These were strange, special joys for the Shear family, culminating in us celebrating by eating on china many times.

Eating on china is one way we love to celebrate the little moments of joy that might otherwise go unnoticed. In fact, Robbie has one of our plates at college, and he eats on it there when we are celebrating something at home.

When I finished writing this book, he sent me a photo of his breakfast sandwich and banana, making a smiley face on china. If you want to feel more joy and less weight of the world, see my video about this tradition, "One Way to Celebrate the Little Things." You can find it on my Joy to the

World Coaching with Robin Shear *YouTube channel.*
(Search @joycoachrobin)

One time, Liza was blocked on the weekend of a huge event I was coordinating at the church, the chili cook-off. This event was our biggest fundraiser for our upcoming teen mission trip to Nicaragua. I had put in months of prep, including a good sixty hours on my feet just that week. I ran all over the building, and my feet were sore.

I know we've veered off into poop,
but this chapter is really about chronic pain.

When it became clear Liza needed an emergency poop walk, we took off on Friday night, despite the pain in my feet.

She didn't go. She was miserable. I gave her more mineral oil, and we went out again the next morning.

Over the course of the weekend, we put in twenty-eight miles of walking.

Eventually, at six a.m. on Sunday, the morning of the chili cook-off, Liza passed the blockage on a walk. I was so happy, I called home to tell everyone she pooped. I have to wonder if anyone overheard that excited phone conversation in the dark and how many times it's been repeated since.

Exhausted, I cleaned up and went to church for worship and the chili cook off. After worship (which included one fun moment when all the Crock-Pots short-circuited the church's electrical system and the organ stopped working in the middle of a hymn), the event was well attended and very busy. I managed a large team of teens and adult volunteers, smiled, had fun, and interacted with everyone, but was secretly in misery the whole time. By the end of the day, my foot pain was excruciating. I was wishing for a stretcher. I had visions of cutting off my own feet.

After the event I rested for a couple of days and propped my feet up, but the pain lingered. Later that week, I returned to walking Liza. I thought the pain would go away like other soreness in the past. It didn't.

I bought new shoes. They were electric purple Adidas shoes with black zigzags, and I was thrilled to wear them even though it felt like I was walking on shards of broken glass, especially in my heels. A couple of weeks passed, and the ongoing pain forced me to see a podiatrist. I was told my awesome new shoes weren't supportive enough and was diagnosed with plantar fasciitis in both feet.

I was like, "But did you see this shade of purple?"

According to the Mayo Clinic,

"Plantar fasciitis is one of the most common causes of heel pain.
It involves inflammation of [the plantar fascia, a band of tissue that runs
across the bottom the foot and connects the heel bone to the toes]. Plantar
fasciitis commonly causes stabbing pain that usually occurs with your first
steps in the morning. As you get up and move, the pain normally decreases,
but it might return after long periods of standing or when you stand up
after sitting. The cause of plantar fasciitis is poorly understood. It is more
common in runners and in people who are overweight."[1] "Most people who
have plantar fasciitis recover in several months with conservative treatment,
such as icing the painful area, stretching, and modifying
or avoiding activities that cause pain."[2]

1   "Plantar Fasciitis: Overview," MayoClinic.org, accessed September 22, 2022, https://www.mayoclinic.org/diseases-conditions/plantar-fasciitis/symptoms-causes/syc-20354846.

2   "Plantar Fasciitis: Diagnosis," MayoClinic.org, accessed September 22, 2022, https://www.mayoclinic.org/diseases-conditions/plantar-fasciitis/diagnosis-treatment/drc-20354851.

Shoot. This meant my walks were going to have to change for a few months.

I am sorry, Liza Jane. I'll make it up to you.

"Okay," I told the doctor. "This is treatable, people get this all the time. What do we have to do to fix it?"

Little did I know it was the beginning of three years of treatment.

By the end, I got so tired of trying to fix this condition that I often doubted it would ever end.

The list of things I tried as recommended by the nine specialists I saw within the first two years included the following:

1. Using $400 custom orthotic insoles in all my shoes.
2. Buying kind of ugly and expensive shoes and sandals from a special shoe store. This happened right when the Payless chain was going out of business, and my feet hurt too bad to stock up on cute, cheap shoes. It seemed like an injustice after all the money I spent there over the years.
3. Wearing hard plastic night splints to hold my feet in a special position while I slept.
4. Steroid injections in the soles of my feet.
5. Three months of physical therapy, three times a week.
6. Three months of ultrasound therapy on my feet.
7. Astym treatment. A therapist basically scraped the soles of my feet with a hard tool to regenerate healthy tissue and break up scar tissue. I could feel and hear the little pockets of inflammation as the tool scraped over them, like bubbles being popped. It killed.
8. Plantar fasciotomy surgery with a second podiatrist. I insisted he operate on both feet on the same day to get it over with. The recovery was interesting. I knew in advance that walking

would be impossible for a few days, so I masterminded a plan for independence. I Superman slid off the bed onto the floor and sat on Robbie's longboard, rolling myself around the house. I was pretty proud of my ingenuity. The kids weren't as impressed. Turns out, seeing me paddling around the house reminded them of a creepy movie, and the twerps made secret videos of me zipping in and out of rooms. *Guys, you're both grounded. For life. Guess you may as well hang out with me!*

9. Several prescription anti-inflammatory medications with all their fun side effects.

10. Oral steroids. The first thing that gave real pain relief, however temporary. It's too bad they aren't safe to use long-term.

11. In addition to standing on soft ice packs to wash dishes and rolling frozen water bottles under my feet every day, I tried six weeks of daily ice dipping to decrease inflammation. This involved submerging my feet and calves for a specified length of time in a five-gallon bucket filled with cold water and big blocks of ice, letting them warm up, and repeating the cycle again and again for thirty minutes. My feet are naturally cold, so I dreaded this one. But it was recommended, and I stuck it out for forty-two days.

12. Using a $150 percussive massager daily. It beat the daylights out of the soles of my feet trying to break up the scar tissue.

13. Ten laser treatments to break up scar tissue at a third doctor's office (a chiropractor).

14. More custom insoles, this time costing $250, from the chiropractor that were softer and supposedly more effective.

15. Rubbing expensive magnesium lotion on my feet daily.

16. Taking a turmeric curcumin supplement for three months.

17. Using a third pair of great-sounding insoles I researched online. The ads made all kinds of promises.

18. Five more months of physical therapy at a new clinic.

19. Five months of electrical stimulation on the soles of my feet at the PT clinic.

20. Five months of WellWave Acoustic Compression (Extracorporeal Shockwave Therapy) at a different PT clinic. "WellWave" sounded nice, and the technician became a lasting friend, but when the shockwaves hit my damaged tissue (with the intention of reigniting my stagnant healing processes), it felt like a machine was driving nails deep into my feet. I had to pray like a crazy woman and imagine Jesus holding my hand to get through this twice a week. Evidently, some people benefit from just a few treatments.

21. The Graston technique. More scraping of my soles to accelerate recovery like they do in the NBA and NFL. *Can I have a championship ring?*

22. Cupping. An ancient form of alternative medicine in which a therapist puts special cups on your skin for a few minutes to create suction. In my case, it was supposed to help with inflammation and blood flow. Remember all the cupping welts on Michael Phelps's back during the 2016 Summer Olympics in Rio? I got to show off cupping welts on my calves and feet. *Does this qualify me for an Olympic medal? Maybe a purple one?*

23. Visceral manipulation. My physical therapist was willing to go to any length to help me, so in addition to a whole lot of other stuff, she tried a manual treatment approach that addresses tension in the soft tissue connections within and around my organs, because tension in one area can be carried through to other regions of the body. She also became a lasting friend. *Cheryl, I'm going to love and appreciate you forever!*

24. Nerve block injections into the soles of my feet by a fourth doctor.

25. A final procedure on each foot: Tenex Ultrasonic
Percutaneous Tenotomy. It removed scar tissue on my
tendons with this little vacuum probe ultrasound wand
inserted in a hole in my foot. It reminded me of the
"Suck Cut" scene from *Wayne's World*. I had heard of this
procedure about a year into the process and had saved
it, just in case it "got that bad." It had "last-ditch hope"
attached to it. This was the procedure I finally broke down
and shared my true feelings about on Facebook.

It didn't work long term. Any of it.

All of this was going on, and almost no one knew. I fought to keep
a smile on my face the whole time. While I was doing my best to be
there for others, I was privately going to a mountain of appointments
and wanting to cut off my feet for three years.

Moral of the story: when someone's not as upbeat as you think they
should be, give them the benefit of the doubt. Assume there is a good
reason.
We can never truly know what some people are privately going through.
Pain is often invisible and very hard to bear emotionally and physically.
Be kind, especially to the grouchiest of people.
Back to you at the studio, Fred.

So, I'd like to have good news to share. Because while the therapies
were interesting, taught me new things, and introduced me to some
wonderful people, overall they didn't help. It seemed that no matter
what I tried, the foot pain persisted.

But as God would have it, I needed to go to a different professional
for something unrelated that you'll read about later. Shockingly,
strategy number 26 was never part of my plantar fasciitis treatment

plan, but about a year later, it changed the entire game, because God is just cool like that: number 26 was EMDR trauma counseling.

Winner winner, chicken dinner!

Wait, really? Counseling fixed a physical problem in my feet? Yes! You better believe it.

In fact, it cured my "incurable" foot pain completely.

I am so thankful to share my story and offer some hope, I will tell you all about it later. I promise.

But for now, it's important that we address the bigger question: how do I choose joy when the pain won't end?

The fact is, there are times when the pain simply won't change. In fact, it may get worse. We can all site personal examples of this.

The pain could be

- Emotional: as in the case of a damaged relationship or a dissatisfying dead-end career.
- Mental: never, ever underestimate the gift of good mental health.
- Spiritual: like when God seems distant, and you wonder if He's hearing your prayers.
- Financial: the inability to meet our basic needs can bring us down to our knees.
- Social: this is all too common, like when isolation and loneliness make us question our worth.
- Physical: the list of possibilities there is endless. God designed us beautifully, yet until Jesus returns, pain exists.

Does any of this sound familiar?

Here's the thing: there's a good chance you read my story wishing you only had to deal with a few years of pain in your feet. You've had it worse.

I am sorry, and I mean no disrespect to your story as I share my own. I want you to know that I almost didn't share this story because I feared it would get the comparisons started. But in sharing our stories, let me remind you that we are in this together. There is hope.

We could minimize our own experiences at the risk of not offending others. It's tempting—and a big part of why I hid my story from the world at large. Here's the however: because we are not in a pain competition and should never allow ourselves to enter one, we need to shrug off the need to compare stories.

This reminds me of a quote you've probably heard by a really wise person (Theodore Roosevelt), and you're about to hear it again now because it's spot-on: "Comparison is the thief of joy."

Go, Teddy! It's so true. You're the man.

Instead, we must acknowledge that pain is pain. An individual can only know his own situation with 100 percent understanding. While my situation may have ended differently than yours, I offer it because it was my experience and it's what I know.

I do have good news for you. Regardless of the depth of pain, I can assure you that joy is possible. It doesn't leave when the chips are down. Why? It was never tied to circumstances in the first place. It was always tied to a way of being, of living, and of viewing the world.

Having said that, we need to talk about grief. If you are in a season of grief, know that it will gradually give way to less burdened feelings. Joy isn't gone; it's just paused, waiting for other feelings to be recognized and heard. The goal is not to rush through grief to get to joy, because grief has purpose. If the "it feels good to feel good" message doesn't feel good right now, know that it's okay. The day will come when it will, little by little. And joy will be waiting for you. Scripture says it best:

**"So with you: Now is your time of grief, but I will see you again
and you will rejoice, and no one will take away your joy."**
(John 16:22)

But let's say that you want to feel joy—you're ready to feel good—
but your situation will not improve. Maybe you have tried everything
you can think of. You might be ready to throw in the towel. Even though
our experiences are different, our feelings are the same.

I'd like to teach you how to choose joy. It's probably simpler than
you'd expect. You see "Choose Joy" on T-shirts and water bottles, but
how?

Choosing joy starts with a question: have you been consciously
adding things to your Joy Bucket List as you read through this book?
Yay you, because guess what? This is the first step.

Sneaky, I know. But now you are off and running!

Awareness is key. Joy is different for everyone, and you won't know
what to choose if you skip this step. Revisit your list. What's on it? What
can you add? What lights you up?

Next, how often are you allowing yourself to choose joy? Do you
feel you have to earn it, or do you give yourself permission to experience
it freely? This is an important question only you can answer. Dig deep.
What comes up?

One simple way to make sure joy is incorporated into your day (and
to give yourself permission to do so, if need be) is to schedule actual joy
breaks. Yup. Permission to play. You can think of them as adult recess
breaks.

It is said that our calendars reflect our priorities. So, do it now:
look at your calendar. What matters to you? Where is joy? Is it on your
schedule often enough?

Read: are you on your schedule often enough?

Even on the most demanding of days, including one or two five-to-ten-minute recess breaks a day can do wonders for your joy bucket. Each break can be unique, depending on what feels good to you in the moment. Ask yourself, *What do I need right now?* Need inspiration? Check your Joy Bucket List! It is waiting to guide you back to *you.*

Take a minute to choose times that work consistently. Add one or two recess breaks to your daily calendar and consider them sacred. Nothing is allowed to interrupt them. They are appointments you've made with yourself. They are an essential part of the day, like brushing your teeth and putting on deodorant.

Tell me you brushed your teeth and put on deodorant today.

For bonus fun points, pick a special ringtone and set it to go off at recess time. It will be something positive to anticipate throughout your day. When that thing plays, you're gone!

The final step is to remain mindful of things that make you feel alive. Add to your Joy Bucket List frequently. Let it be an active document, always growing and changing, something you think about often. Talk to people about what brings them joy. Join my private Facebook group, where we focus on sources of joy on purpose. It's called—wait for it—The Joy Bucket. You can search for it on Facebook and join.

As simple as it sounds, whether it's spontaneous or scheduled, simply focusing on joy can change your outlook and help you see the most painful day through a more positive lens. Joy won't change your circumstances, but it will change how you view them. It's all about perspective and perseverance.

So, for a quick review, if you want to choose joy, even on the most challenging of days,

- know where it comes from,
- be mindful of your list when you need it,
- take recess breaks on a regular basis,
- and keep adding to your list.

If you need a partner to work through the specifics, reach out to me anytime at joytotheworldcoaching.com.

And when you see someone wearing a "Choose Joy" T-shirt, ask them if they know the steps. Then buy yourself a shirt.

The great thing is, as simple as it sounds, choosing joy works. Because gratitude brings me joy, incorporating it intentionally that day in the ER brought me crazy amounts of joy in an unexpected situation.

Let me give you another example of a time I was having a tough day and what happened when I intentionally chose joy . . . because it includes you.

One day, about two years into my attempt at foot pain relief, I remember needing to take a break and rest. My feet were killing me and making me cranky. I was working my way through an intense portion of life coaching school, running around the house (with arch support shoes on, as I couldn't walk barefoot, even in the shower), and taking care of random things while we were on a class break.

I sat down on a big round chair in our sunroom to rest and pray. The sun was pouring in from above, and I let myself pause long enough to soak up its beautiful warmth. Just before the break, we were told that the time had come to consider what direction we wanted to go with our life coaching.

Gosh. Did I want to help people with their health? Finances? Careers? There were so many options.

It just so happened, that morning I began my second round of physical therapy, the round that became a five-month commitment and included the electric shock treatment. My feet hurt so bad I expected to see red, throbbing cartoon feet when I looked at them, like a Looney Tunes character who had pianos dropped on them from a cliff.

It was one of those "I want to chop off my feet" moments.

That's when it hit me.

Joy beats pain every time. Joy was something I knew. Something I had seen help my family, people with eating disorders, stressed-out teens, and lonely senior citizens.

It seemed like the perfect day to begin my joy coaching business.

Yup, I was in pain, but I was going to focus on joy . . . big-time. Why would I want to dwell on my lousy circumstances when I knew that other people were out there, hurting, just like me?

When I knew that *you* were out there, needing this message?

It occurred to me that I was uniquely gifted to help people find joy. God dumped it in my heart for a reason, and it sure as heck wasn't so I could keep it to myself. Just the thought of being able to make a difference made me so excited, I forgot my feet hurt at all. Before long, I was dancing in the kitchen with the cat to "Uptown Funk," thankful. Mickey was less thankful.

> **"You turned my wailing into dancing; you removed**
> **my sackcloth and clothed me with joy."**
> *(Psalm 30:11)*

I was hurting, then chose joy, and here we are together.

The thing is, even if you don't want to hock joy for a living, simply focusing on adding more of it to your life can change your outlook when life is messy. There are times when this is the last thing you feel like doing—when you must force yourself to choose joy—and I pray you do it anyway.

It won't change your circumstances, but it will change the way you view them.

But what about the times you don't choose it and it bubbles up out of nowhere anyway? It comes unexpectedly and you don't know why. One minute you're in the dumps and the next you're laughing harder than you have laughed in months?

Sometimes, my friend, joy is a gift from the Lord. Say thank you! God is giving it to you.

"But the fruit of the Spirit is love, joy, peace, forbearance, kindness, goodness, faithfulness, gentleness and self-control."
(Galatians 5:22–23)

We never know when God is going to bless us with the gift of joy. Stay connected to the Holy Spirit, and let Him fill you with joy anytime He wants.

Now, to all my type A homies, if you are hoping to predict God's next move and make plans accordingly, I hate to say it, but the joke's on you. You need to let it go.

Anyone want me to sing the Disney song? Say no.
Or Meghan Trainor? Also no.

God is entirely full of surprises. The whole EMDR therapy curing my foot pain thing is a great example. Who knew? God was giving me the gift of joy. In my opinion, God's unpredictability is one of His best qualities. Why would we want a God who only does things we expect or pray for when we can have one who surprises us with His blessings when we least expect them? We don't have to know what He's going to do and when. The only thing we need to know for sure is that God is good. That's more than enough. Let that sink in and fill up your joy bucket.

The psalmist says it best:

"Weeping may endure for a night, but joy cometh in the morning."
(Psalm 30:5 KJV)

God Himself will decide when morning will come, and at times the night will last for years and seem like it will never end, as you'll see in my next story.

Exhaling. This one is the whopper, the big kahuna.

But morning will come. When it does, all I can say is, have Bruno Mars in the queue, my friend.

Because joy will come with it.

Messy Joy Spill-Your-Guts Journal Questions:

1. What long-term, painful situations have you experienced in your lifetime?

2. As you look back on those experiences, what lessons come up for you? What advice would you have for your younger self?

3. Name a friend you met because of a difficult situation.

4. My story of privately being in pain is a reminder that there may be more going on than meets the eye. How can you remember to give grace to people who are less than kind, not knowing what they are secretly experiencing?

5. Has God ever surprised you with unexpected healing? What happened?

6. In your understanding, where is joy when your pain won't end?

7. As you look at your life right now, what types of pain seem present? Which is most persistent? What might help?

8. Can you think of times you were tempted to compare your pain to the things other people were experiencing? What effect did this have on you? Did it affect the other person in any way? How did it affect the amount of joy in your life?

9. Look at your sources of joy on your Joy Bucket List. Which, if any, are tied to circumstances? Do they belong on the list, or are they sources of happiness?

10. Do you allow yourself to feel joy freely, or do you believe you need to earn it? Why?

11. How diligent are you about focusing on the things that make you feel most alive, making sure to schedule them into your day?

12. In terms of joy, what's your sweet spot—the optimal number of times each week that joy is scheduled into your calendar? Why? And how long should your joy breaks last?

13. Can you think of a time when choosing joy changed your outlook, despite your circumstances? Tell the story and what you learned.

14. Share your thoughts about times when God gave you the gift of joy when you least expected it.

15. How do you feel about God being full of surprises? Do you find Him predictable?

16. Write about a time when you especially related to the words of Psalm 30:5.

CHAPTER 11

If I Bury My Head in the Sand Long Enough, Will It Go Away?

So, here's the truth: I was hiding more than foot pain from the world at large. More than gut pain. Even more than head pain. I was hiding emotional pain from trauma experienced decades earlier.

Life was as messy as could be, and I kept smiling, helping people find joy, avoiding my own truth.

Before I even tell you the story, in case you don't make it to the end of the chapter, I'll give you the answer to the title right here and now: no.

Burying your head in the sand—no matter how long—will not make it go away.

Whew. This is a hard one. This is the one I never wanted to tell.

You know how we sometimes experience things that are so awful, we don't want anyone to know they happened? And we don't even want to admit to ourselves that they happened?

I am praying like crazy as I write this because I am about to share one of those stories. The event didn't happen by choice, and sharing it isn't by choice either. But because it's relevant to other experiences in this book, things I know God wants me to share, I believe that He wants this one included too. Sharing this is about obedience and trust.

I need to say, out of love to anyone who has experienced any type of trauma: if you actively avoid triggers, this might be a chapter for you to skip until you are ready. I hope you're getting the help you need. I love you.

Okay, here goes: A straightforward story of an event that changed my life . . . and thankfully, one that God was very present in. And eventually, one that joy was found in.

When I was about fourteen, I was a cheerleader.

Hard to imagine, I know.

I loved it. Cheering was a great energy outlet, good for my health and so much fun to boot. One of the main reasons I cheered was to be with my friends. We had a blast at practices, sleepovers, and hanging out after practice.

Picture a bunch of chattering teen girls with bad '80s hair and puffy-sleeved shirts pretending to understand football well enough to holler out the right cheers at the right time. Really all we wanted to do was goof around, eat gravy-covered fries at Lou Lou's before games, wear the uniforms, ride the team bus, and talk about boys. It was great.

Practice was right after school. We sometimes congregated in a balcony off the gym after practice ended, not ready to go home, just being girls. We didn't cause any trouble, but we just wanted more time together.

One day in school, I noticed a few of the football players whispering and looking at me and some of the other cheerleaders in class. Now, these were guys we had known practically from birth. We grew up in a tiny town where everybody knew everybody. We knew each other's siblings, parents, and grandparents. All of my friends called Patty's grandma "The Food Grandma," and my grandpa was affectionately known as "The Fart Grandpa."

I am sorry, Grandpa. This isn't the most reputable way to honor your memory, especially when you meant so much to me.
But, come on, you earned it! I am laughing as I type.
Even now, your comedic timing is perfect. Thank you.

So, yeah, imagine growing up in a town with one flashing yellow light. One gas station. No chain restaurants. A village that is still struggling to maintain a comma in its official population count. The small-town vibe provided safety. There was security in knowing people.

Or so we thought.

Back to the whispering boys in class. Of course, I saw and heard them, and asked what was going on. I distinctly remember one saying, "You'll know after practice." The memory of it haunts me to this day.

"You'll know after practice."

Knowing them like I did, I laughed it off in the moment, assuming they were up to something stupid as usual.

Boy was I right.

Whew.
How about that Spartan basketball program?

The school day ended, and we went to practice. As usual, we girls hung out in the balcony for a bit afterward. That's when we heard the footsteps. As I live and breathe, I can still hear rambunctious voices and the sound of feet quickly pounding the stairs. The boys. Coming our way.

I will not use this platform to identify the boys. That is not at all the purpose of my sharing. Please know my heart here.

Like many victims, for reasons I don't understand, I have protected them my whole life.

And, even if I wanted to share their names, I couldn't. It was so painful, I have repressed the faces of all the boys, all but two. I couldn't identify the rest if I tried. So, there's that.

Everything happened so fast. It was a blur. What I remember with clarity was seeing a group of boys running full speed at us. Of course, we took off. I didn't think much of it. Maybe they were going to catch us and tickle us? Give us noogies? Wet willies? They were our friends.

The other girls were faster than I was. They grabbed their bags and took off down the stairs on the other side of the balcony, screaming, laughing. I can still hear their laughter. Their feet.

My feet didn't make it to the stairs.

The next thing I knew, the boys had me down on the floor. The wrestling team practiced in the balcony, and their gigantic, thick, stinky black mat was down. I can still smell the disgusting dried sweat on that thing.

The memory turns my stomach even now.

Soon, I was pinned down. Hands were grabbing me everywhere. This was no innocent tickle fest. I would have killed for a wet willie. No, this was something different.

I remember a blur of bodies, hands, arms, boys. Boys without faces. I remember screaming. Yelling for help. Fighting for my life.

I distinctly remember that one boy stood off to the side. He chose not to participate. As thankful as I was for his decision to do me no harm, he also chose not to help me . . . essentially harming me. Oh, how I wish I could see his face. I wish I could ask him why he didn't do something. He literally stood there, leaning against the balcony railing while I cried for help.

Doing nothing.

So, thanks be to God, and I mean that with the utmost sincerity, here's the part where my story improves dramatically. Somehow, some way, I managed to get out from under all the testosterone and muscle. To this day I don't know how . . . but I got out of there.

Here's what I know for sure: I am currently five foot two on a good day. The snow pants I ski in were bought in the kids' section. So it makes no sense that the even-smaller fourteen-year-old me had the strength to free herself from a mass of hormonal football players. This is how I know that it had to be God. There is no other explanation.

You might be reading this, remembering your own trauma (by Google definition, a deeply distressing or disturbing experience), wondering where God was. What we can know is that God was very much there, providing escape in other ways. Sin hurts His heart. He hates it. As Proverbs 6:16–19 (ESV) says, "There are six things that the LORD hates, seven that are an abomination to him: haughty eyes, a lying tongue, and hands that shed innocent blood, a heart that devises wicked plans, feet that make haste to run to evil, a false witness who breathes out lies, and one who sows discord among brothers." Know that pain was never God's plan. It won't always be this way. But until God's plan is restored, He can use our pain for good. I have a whole chapter dedicated to this truth . . . please don't quit reading because you wonder if God was with you. He was. He is. Instead, I pray that you reread chapter 6 of this book and that you trust God anyway, even if you don't understand why bad things happened to you.

So, at this point, I took off running as fast as I can. Thankfully, I can still hear the sound of my own feet on those stairs. The feet that helped me get the hell out of there, physically unharmed.

We lived less than a mile from school, and I ran all the way home. I have never run so fast in my life. I was sobbing, hyperventilating, devastated.

And then I saw my shorts. As if things weren't bad enough, when I got about halfway home and looked down, I realized my shorts were ripped all the way up to the waistband on one side. They were flopping open as I ran, underwear showing for the world to see, and I had no idea. The entire town could have seen me running, in this crazed state, snot everywhere, panties visible. People's grandparents could have been watching.

And you know what my biggest fear was? That they would have judged me as someone who asked for it.

Anyone who's been victimized will understand the insanity in my thinking.

Again, if that's you and you're still here with me now, hear me out:
It was not your fault. You did not choose to be a victim.
I love you. I mean it.

Recognizing my fear of judgment was a horrifying moment that smacked me so hard emotionally it stands out vividly in my memory. There are times when that exact spot on the road pops up so clearly in my mind, and my heart instantly races . . . afraid of what people will think.

Dang it, I hate this story. Are you sure, God?
Help me breathe.

When I got home, I burst through the garage door and crumpled into a crying heap at the dining room table as I told my mom what happened. I cried so hard; I am amazed she understood my words at all.

Astounded, enraged, she immediately called the principal and reported the attempted group rape.

I didn't tell my sister, Tracy. I didn't tell her until I was in my midforties. She had no idea. I just told my dad for the first time after signing on my book deal. It's not the kind of thing I wanted to talk about.

I don't remember talking about it anymore at home that night. Or ever again at home.

But I do remember going to school the next day.

Messy Joy Spill-Your-Guts Journal Questions:

1. As you read this chapter, if something you've buried came to mind, write about it here.

2. If the above question applied to you, what effect has burying it had on you?

3. I shared the story of my attempted group rape experience out of obedience and trust. Write about some times you chose to be obedient and trust God, even when it was scary.

4. Are you surprised that joy can be found in this particular story, years later? What difficulties have you experienced that took years to lead to joy, but led to it nonetheless?

5. When you think back about your toughest experiences, who was there to support you? What difference did their presence make in your life? If possible, how might you make them aware of the impact they had on you?

6. I shared how I found false security in knowing many people in my small town. What have you found false security in? What have you found true security in?

7. Is there someone you have protected who has caused you pain in some way? Why might that be? How does protecting that person add to or detract from the amount of joy in your life?

8. Can you think of a time when something good happened that you were in no way capable of without God's help?

9. How has fear of judgment held you back from healing? Other than judgment, what are you afraid of? What effect has this had on the joy in your life?

10. What have you learned about God's presence during your darkest times? What Bible verses speak truth into your situation?

CHAPTER 12

Do I Need To Go to Therapy?

"Did you hear what happened?"

Rumors were swirling everywhere. Kids talked, big-time. In a small town, everyone talks about each other's business. There's not much else to do.

Seeing those boys at school the next day was awful. I wanted to crawl in a closet. I wanted to die.

Before first hour ended, the principal's voice came over the loudspeaker. Heard by the entire student body, our names were read, and we were asked to come to the office.

Mortified, the rumors were confirmed right then and there.

I am shaking my head as I type this. There's so much about this story that should have been different.

I dragged myself to the office, wanting to be invisible, trying not to throw up, wishing I could die, and found myself face-to-face with all my attackers. And their parents.

Wouldn't you know it, my parents weren't there.

When I brought this meeting up to my mom recently, she was surprised. She knew nothing of it. To this day we don't know why she wasn't informed about it, even though she worked in the next building over.

In the office we had a conversation about our versions of what happened, guided by the principal. The boys defended themselves, but not as vehemently as their parents did. The parents I can see in my memory were power players in our town. Their kids excelled at sports. Their boys were the good kids. The heroes. The small-town gods.

Yeah, you can guess how this is going to end.

I couldn't look anyone in the eye. I felt so alone, so small, so targeted, so very unheard. I looked down the whole time. I can still see the pattern of my chair's ugly fabric in my mind. It felt like wool, and the memory of its scratchiness makes my skin crawl. I cringe at the mental image of the cheap swirly yellow wood grain on the arms. That chair was all I had. I should have been thankful for it, but in all honesty I have imagined taking an axe to it so many times.

The boys were let off the hook. For them the experience was over. The smug looks on the faces of the two boys I can identify will be forever burned in my mind. They were my friends.

I became voiceless.

For the rest of the year, and for all the years leading up to graduation, I had to face those boys every single day.

And for survival I had to pretend to be okay and even pretend to be their friend. It didn't matter that I was secretly suicidal. In public I projected confidence and peace.

I didn't go to therapy. It wasn't suggested, and it sure wasn't on my radar as an option. So I buried it. Deep. So deep that I barely thought about it. I planned to get away without addressing it. The memory was boxed up tight, mentally covered with duct tape, tucked away in a dark closet of my mind, out of sight. Dealt with.

Or so I thought.

Years later, as a young married mom, I ran a private nutrition counseling practice at a doctor's office. A registered nutritionist/dietitian, I saw mostly clients who had deadly eating disorders. Oh, how I loved my clients. I am still privileged to mentor some of them to this day.

Most of them had backgrounds as sexual trauma victims, which they used their eating disorder to escape from. They shared their stories. My heart bled for them.

And that's when my night terrors began.

I only ran that business for five years, but for a total of twenty-one years, at random times, I bolted upright in my sleep, screaming so loudly that it woke the kids up on the other side of the house. Not to mention my poor husband. Did I mention he's a saint?

Rick Shear, you deserve an award. You really do.

For too many nights to count, I was locked in a state of sheer panic, terrified that a faceless man was in my room, intending harm. The terror of "seeing" him stand next to the bed without being able to escape made me shake violently enough to wake me up, again and again. Often, I didn't remember having the dream until someone in the family told me the next day that they'd heard me scream. Sometimes the reality would hit me a couple of days later. And the panic would come back, even in the daytime.

I was so afraid it would happen when one of the kids had a friend over. We hosted countless slumber parties over the years. We always loved providing a space where the kids and their friends enjoyed being. We decided early on as young parents that our home would be a place where kids gravitated. The whole night-terror, screaming-in-my-sleep thing didn't fit real well with that.

I was exhausted. The dreams would usually strike the second I drifted off for the night, leaving me afraid to go back to sleep. Rest is so important for every single cell in our bodies. Fearing rest was no way to live.

The last thing I wanted to do was actually talk about what I had experienced so many years earlier. I would rather saw off my own arm with a nail file.

Are you having as much fun with these illustrations as I am?

But I had proof it wasn't going to get better on its own. It was getting worse. So I found a trauma counselor—the one I mentioned earlier who helped me so much with my TBI head trash. In fact, this was why I had a counselor in the first place—and I began therapy and was quickly diagnosed with PTSD.

That's a new one, a joy coach with PTSD!
What will they think of next?
Here's a little love for my type A peeps: now that you know
the whole story, this is a fun timeline of the pieces of my story
chronologically, because I know you like things orderly:
Coped with foot pain for two and a half years
Started a joy coaching business from the ground up
Began EMDR trauma counseling for sexual assault
from years earlier
Started skiing, with foot pain
Eventually, counseling had the side benefit
of freeing my feet from pain
Ski injury caused concussion
Treated for Candida overgrowth and had psychotic episode
Heard from The Holy Spirit it was time to open up
and share Messy Joy

My counselor was trained in a special therapeutic technique known as EMDR. This was essential to me, as I had heard many EMDR success stories from my clients with eating disorders over the years. The term EMDR stands for Eye Movement Desensitization and Reprocessing. You can read all about it on www.emdr.com, but basically it involves bilateral (two-sided) stimulation while short segments of painful memories are shared and reprocessed. Originated and developed by

Dr. Francine Shapiro, the way I understand it, EMDR makes both sides of the brain play nice together after trauma creates a disconnect. Connected brains allow for healing and moving on. These are very simplified terms which I am sure would make any therapist shudder.

Therapists, you can write your own book
and redefine joy just to get even.

When I first heard of EMDR from my clients, I thought it sounded like a joke. Why would moving eyes, holding buzzing remotes, listening to a rhythmic ticking sound, or tapping on shoulders back and forth have any effect on the way someone viewed their trauma? Honestly, I have no idea. But it worked for them.

As odd as the whole bilateral stimulation thing sounded to me, I proceeded, because there were several studies to back EMDR's effectiveness and safety. According to EMDR Institute, "There has been so much research on EMDR therapy that it is now recognized as an effective form of treatment for trauma and other disturbing experiences by organizations such as the American Psychiatric Association, the World Health Organization and the Department of Defense."[3]

And you know what? It worked for me too.

The first time I realized it was working, it came as a complete surprise. Roughly a few months in, at about the three-year point in my chronic foot pain journey, I took a walk and realized my feet felt fine.

I took a walk and realized my feet felt fine!
What in the world?!

I'd heard people proclaim the wonders of the mind-body connection, but it never occurred to me that plantar fasciitis could be cured by talking

---

3   "What Is EMDR?," EMDR.com, accessed August 18, 2022, https://www.emdr.com/what-is-emdr/.

about my trauma. As ludicrous as it seemed, I should have known better. Years earlier, I had experienced the power of the mind-body connection for myself (in short, chronic back pain wasn't relieved by PT or opiates, but asking myself, "Is something bothering me?" did relieve it. This was based on Dr. John Sarno's research in his book *Healing Back Pain*). For some reason—maybe I belong in the "ignorance is bliss" category with my grandma—it never dawned on me that acknowledging the role my mind might be playing in perpetuating the pain cycle could have helped my feet.

Had I thought to give proper credit where credit was due, I could have felt better and been in cute shoes much, much earlier.

But gosh, I was thankful and dancing for joy, because my foot pain was cured entirely by EMDR therapy. Entirely. Sadly, Liza Jane had died about two years earlier, but I could hardly contain my exuberance as I returned to walking for both of us. I went as far as I wanted, remembering our great times together, all while wearing those awesome electric purple Adidas shoes. I pounded the pavement until the treads were smooth, grateful the whole time.

And eventually, EMDR made my PTSD night terrors stop (for the most part).

Now I can tell people my trauma story without completely falling apart. The first time I shared my story was with a live audience. About a year into EMDR therapy, while I was recovering from my head injury, I was asked to speak at a virtual summit. The subject of sharing our stories to empower ourselves and help others open up really appealed to me I gratefully accepted the opportunity to speak and planned to share a completely different story about the importance of sharing your hurts even if you think they don't compare to others'.

But EMDR had set me free and suddenly, I felt the urge to share my attack and healing story with a room full of strangers. I was so scared I'd bawl my way through it, I held tightly to a wad of tissues. When the story poured out, I was so relieved to have made it through the story, offered others hope, and done it without tears, I celebrated by throwing my wad of dry Kleenex right at the camera. It felt incredible!

There was comfort in being able to say the words. There was comfort in knowing I was safe. There was comfort because no one in the audience knew my attackers.

I knew then that God was calling me to write this book, but I never thought I'd be able to include these chapters. Writing books tends to open doors for speaking opportunities, and the fact is, as much as I love to speak to audiences, writing this means the boys or their parents may read it. Or they may be in one of my audiences.

I hate the thought of this bringing up something they'd rather not think about. All these years later, at times I still want to protect my attackers.

But enough time has passed that my voice has returned. I will not remain silent.

God has given me strength, and He will offer it to them if that's what they need after hearing about this. I have prayed for them many times and believe He will be merciful to them if they ask for forgiveness. I hope they do.

In all honesty, it's such a relief to get this out. I have started and deleted these two chapters so many times in the course of writing this book. It just hurt too much to share. Every time I started to write them, the night terrors returned. The old fear of judgment crept back in, as did fear that rumors would circulate in my small town (aka "The Big O"), where I still live with my family to this day.

Go, Big O!
You're A-W-E-S-O-M-E,
you're awesome, you're awesome . . . like totally.
Work with me, people, it was the '80s.

Life is full of surprises. Never in a million years did I imagine I would want to share this. I didn't even plan to write this today. Yet for some reason—undoubtedly by the peace of the Holy Spirit—the words flowed. I felt queasy at times as I typed and had a headache throughout, but I am okay.

I am okay!

The words are out. They tell my story. It happened. I will no longer feel the need to keep it buried inside. The world can judge me any way it wishes. I know my innocence, and I can't control the world's opinions.

What about you? If a joy coach can have PTSD and need EMDR, maybe others can too. Perhaps we are in this together.

If you've experienced trauma—again, that's what experts call a deeply distressing or disturbing experience—burying your head in the sand will not make it go away. Ignoring it will make it eventually come back, with a vengeance.

There's no joy in that.

However, talking about it with a therapist or counselor might help you heal. You might even benefit from EMDR therapy. One way to find a therapist trained in EMDR is to visit the "Find a Therapist" tab on Psychology Today's website. Without entering your city or zip, click the search icon instead. When the new page opens, scroll down and click on your state. If you'd like to find an EMDR-certified therapist, choose "EMDR" from the "Types of Therapy" tab.

Let me encourage you to do the work. No, it won't be fun. It won't be easy. But you are worth it. Your freedom is waiting.

Another very important thing you can do is talk with a pastor about forgiveness.

While I never thought I'd share this story, neither did I imagine I would want to forgive my attackers. And that's when I knew an even greater joy. Read on to hear more about my forgiveness journey and see if there might be a message for you as well.

Messy Joy Spill-Your-Guts Journal Questions:

1. God gave me strength to escape, face my attackers at school, and heal. Take all the time you need to give God praise for the times He has given you strength, to your knowledge. May this take several sheets of paper and a long, long time.

2. I wanted to die rather than face my attackers. What advice or encouragement would you have for someone who feels like this? Is there a story behind your answer?

3. Because so many people are hurting and alone today, how can you be more aware of what people you love are really thinking and feeling?

4. What would you like your loved ones to know about how you are currently doing? About a hurt you experienced in the past?

5. Can you think of a time you felt completely alone, like I did in the school office? How did you get through it? Where was God?

6. Have you ever felt voiceless? If so, write about it here. Were you able to find your voice? If so, how?

7. Is there a story that you need to share but you fear someone will be villainized? Share it here. What might God be trying to tell you?

8. How are your sleep habits? How does the quality of your sleep tie in to the amount of joy in your life? Is this something you've ever given thought to before?

9. If you need better sleep, what are three things you can change this week to make that possible?

10. Look back on the most difficult experiences of your life. Given the definition of trauma (a deeply distressing or disturbing experience), do you believe you've processed those trials in a way that allows you to feel healed? If not, what are your thoughts about seeking professional help?

11. Have you ever been to counseling? Write about your experience. What effect did it have on the level of joy in your life?

12. It took me many years, but I finally learned to find my voice regarding my trauma. If there's a time you found your voice again, write about your experience here. What effect did finding your voice have on the level of joy in your life?

13. Most of us know someone who's struggling silently. What advice do you have for him or her?

CHAPTER 13

Forgiveness and Joy— Is There A Connection?

**"Be kind and compassionate to one another,
forgiving each other, just as in Christ God forgave you."**
(Ephesians 4:32)

I wonder, do my attackers still think about what they did? Are they sorry? Have they prayed for forgiveness? Do they have different perspectives as fathers and warn their daughters about the kinds of boys they used to be? I have no idea. I have most likely seen them at sporting events and class reunions, but we have never talked about it.

The boys did not show me kindness or compassion. But the thing is, I cannot control the decisions of other people. I can only control my own actions. The Lord has shown me kindness, compassion, and forgiveness when I did not deserve it. I can choose to extend the same to them. I need to. God commands it.

By God's grace, the day came that I did want to forgive them. They don't know it, but that's okay. It was as much for me as it was for them.

And the best part is, that was the day I realized just how directly forgiveness ties into joy.

As it happened, one morning I was lying in bed, not even thinking about my trauma, shortly after sharing my Kleenex-throwing story at the summit, when it became clear to me that I was ready to forgive them. It hit me out of the blue. It wasn't a forced, required thing. I suddenly had so much peace around the idea, it made no sense . . . yet it made sense. It had to be coming from God.

> **"And the peace of God, which transcends all understanding, will guard your hearts and your minds in Christ Jesus."**
> *(Philippians 4:7)*

Yeah, this peace transcended my ability to understand for sure.

Sure enough, God was helping me then like He helped me after school that day, like He helped me graduate without killing myself, like He helped me relax and sleep after every night terror, and like He helped me find professional help. Like He is helping me share this now.

After more than thirty years of feeling angry and robbed by the way my life was impacted by one momentary decision a bunch of impulsive boys had made, just like that, with a breath, I let go of my anger. The pain was gone. Forgiving them in a time of prayer made me feel amazing. It was freeing. I felt joyful and giddy for the rest of the day. And the next.

I remember texting Tracy and my mom after I'd prayed, overjoyed. We have a group chat that often becomes grounds for GIF wars. I said, "I just want you to know I have forgiven my attackers. I am so thankful, I feel like I could fly!"

My mom said, "That's great! I am so happy for you! Just don't go up on the roof."

As if.

As great as it felt to forgive my attackers, strangely I wasn't free. There was more work to be done. There was someone else I needed to forgive.

My mom.

I need to preface this by saying that I have been blessed from the beginning with a very loving mom. My mom would do anything for anyone. She always shows up when people are in need with some token of love, often in plastic grocery bags.

Love you, Mom!
I may be teasing about the bags, but I am sincere about the love.

I am going to share my experience and my view of things, but I do this without placing blame on anyone. It's hard for me to share this part because I would never want anyone to feel attacked. But because this story is pivotal to my message of finding joy in the mess, I include it, praying my heart and intentions are clear. My mom read these chapters in advance of my decision to include them.

So, as loving as my mom was, we were often at different places emotionally. We are generally on opposite ends of the emotional pool. I gravitate toward the deep end: I feel things completely and like to talk about my feelings, processing them and picking them apart. To make it even more fun, I also feel other people's feelings completely. I'm an empath.

While my mom is very caring, she likes to keep her feelings pretty tidy. When she cries, it's a bigger deal and she tends to point out the fact that it happened, whereas I cry watching commercials and hope no one sees. My mom has a harder time talking about the more emotional subjects. She's still in the water, but in the shallow end. We both swim, but differently.

When I was in first grade, my dad moved out. Being in a house with odd numbers led to me often feeling left out. No one did it intentionally, and no, I do not need to be the center of attention, but I do need to feel included. To this day, when I don't, I struggle.

*Even now, I like to sit between family members at church,
never on the end, because I like to be a part of the conversation
before worship starts. Rick thinks this is funny, but he always
arranges things so I can sit in the middle.*

We had a lot of fun moments and made great memories at home, but when there are odd numbers of people, chances are, someone is going to run the risk of feeling left out. Especially someone who feels things deeply and has a strong need to be included.

*I needed to be included so badly as a child,
I'd intentionally slow down on bike rides with my sister and neighborhood
friends in hopes that they'd miss me. Yeah, I was that kid.
Wanna ride? I promise, I don't do that anymore.*

I think my mom wanted me to develop tougher skin and be "less emotional," so she tried to help me believe that things weren't a big deal, when to me they were. Feeling left out was definitely one of those things.

As it is in many families, people can be cut from the same cloth. In our family, my mom and sister were those people. They saw many things the same way, and their personalities really meshed well. They often seemed more like sisters than parent and child. My personality jived with those of my dad and grandpa, who didn't live with us. So there were a lot of times when I felt like a misfit at home. Like I didn't belong. Like there wasn't a connection. Like there must be something wrong with me.

My feelings of being different were so strong, I wondered if I was adopted from another family. I can remember a few times when no one was looking, I'd open up my mom's files and look for my adoption papers. I'd quickly rifle through the drawer, looking for proof, because surely I must have had another family somewhere. Otherwise, there would have been more of a sense of connection, of belonging, of similarity.

While we laughed a lot at home, much of the time, I felt like I needed to change to fit in.

I was dying for someone to recognize my emotions as a good thing. For someone to talk about my feelings with. I was longing for deep conversations about the bigger things in life. Instead, I was told I was "sensitive" and "too emotional" and that things that bothered me were "fine."

But when I was attacked in the balcony in middle school, I was grateful my mom was there for me. She jumped into action that night without missing a beat. I knew she was on my side, and it made a world of difference in a time when I would have otherwise felt very, very alone.

However, to my recollection, we never talked about it at home again.

All of those thoughts, all of those memories and fears and feelings . . . they got boxed up and tucked away in the back corner of my mind, nearly forgotten forever.

Fast-forward to adulthood. Night terrors were happening on a regular basis. I didn't say anything about them to my mom for a long time. While I didn't want to worry her, I also didn't want to be told that it was fine, that I needed to shake them off and quit being so sensitive.

But after a few years, I finally broke down and told her about them. She didn't ask why they were happening. I assumed she knew.

When enough was enough and I knew it was time to try to solve the root issue behind the nightmares, I sought the help I wrote about earlier.

Making the decision to see a trauma therapist was monumental because after all those years, I was still uncertain if my situation was considered "trauma," since I got away. (It was.) My whole life, I wondered if I was making a big deal out of nothing. (I wasn't.) Nothing physically harmful happened. Did that mean everything was "fine" and I was reacting to nothing? (No.)

Was I fixed on this just to get attention?

When I finally got up the guts to schedule my first EMDR therapy session, I decided to tell my mom about it.

Of course, she was glad to hear I was getting help for the nightmares. She didn't want me to suffer. She asked, "What kind of counselor are you seeing?" to which I nervously admitted, "A trauma counselor."

I can point out the exact spot where we were driving in her car when she asked, "Why a trauma counselor? It's not like you've ever experienced any trauma."

"Mom, I am pretty sure that the sexual attack in middle school counts as trauma."

She wondered what sexual attack I was talking about.

I briefly recounted the story, this horrible thing that I had both remembered and forcefully forgotten too many times to count, to which she replied, "Oh, I forgot about that."

I can point out that spot in the road too.

We were about an hour and a half from home. The pain caused by that simple statement was so intense, I seriously considered asking her to pull over so I could get out of the car and walk home. It didn't matter that my feet were killing me. It wasn't me thinking dramatically. It was a survival thought.

I felt like an animal in a cage for the rest of the ride home, heart pounding, struggling to breathe.

I had all the feels, and I couldn't talk about them.

We didn't speak of this conversation again.

I spent the next year of therapy working through not only the actual trauma experience itself but also the pain of that one moment with her and how it seemed to confirm my childhood feelings and fears that I didn't matter.

Over the course of that counseling year, as much as I loved my mom and as much as I knew she loved me, I could hardly be in her presence. I wanted an apology so badly that it was all I could think of when we were together. All other subjects seemed shallow and unimportant by comparison. I couldn't engage. It was the first year of the COVID-19 pandemic, and protecting her from the virus became a convenient excuse.

I knew it was hurting her that I wasn't around, and I felt terrible about it. Tracy brought it up often and pleaded with me to work out whatever was going on with Mom. I couldn't explain it to either of them.

Since we couldn't talk about this thing that really mattered to me, and I couldn't find peace in her presence, I kept my distance. And kept going to EMDR therapy.

And along the way, I found out about the *Candida* thing and went skiing and hit my head.

I didn't share any of what was going on publicly, but it was a fun year.

In truth it was a nightmare.

Because my mom is very action-oriented, she was awesome when I was recovering from the concussion. True to form, she showed up often with tokens of love in plastic bags. She made dinner. She brought over goodies. She called and texted frequently to make sure I was resting and not overdoing it.

Without a doubt, I knew that my mom was truly concerned about me. The one who usually said everything was "fine" was really showing her feelings. Worry. Fear. Uncertainty. It was obvious.

She clearly wanted to do anything she could to help me get better.

That's when, a few months into my recovery, I wasn't driving and needed frequent rides to physical therapy and acupuncture, the only person I could ask was my mom. All my other family members were working or going to school. I had spent a whole year trying to avoid her and protect my heart, and now we were going to be in a car together twice a week for several hours.

Wasn't this just like God?

Here's how I know God was the one behind it all.

Because it didn't make sense otherwise how those car rides turned out to be an absolute gift. Why was my mom suddenly

- extra in touch with my needs?
- letting me talk about my feelings?
- asking me questions about things that I had always longed to talk about?
- open to discussing big subjects, things with really deep meaning, without shutting me down and talking about trivial, safe things instead?

Because God is good and can use our biggest messes for the greatest joy.

Read that again.

God is good and can use our biggest messes for the greatest joy.

Before long I looked forward to those rides. My walls were coming down. I jokingly referred to my mom as "Driving Miss Daisy." We ate out, laughed, sang songs, told stories, had fun . . . we connected.

We connected!

One time, on a country road between the back-to-back appointments about an hour apart, we laughed until we threw our heads back and snorted. Tears were rolling down our cheeks. My mom was laughing so hard, she pounded the steering wheel. I have no idea what we were laughing about, but I will always, always remember the way it felt.

It felt amazing. It felt like joy.

That's a spot on a road I'm grateful to have a memory of.

About a month into all of this time together, it was Mother's Day. For the first time ever, I stood in the greeting card aisle, having a hard time choosing a Mother's Day card. I struggled not because our relationship was lacking but because it was so rich, there were too many perfect cards to choose from. I bought more than one.

As a gift, I made her "Driving Miss Daisy" movie tickets, which were only redeemable at my house, with lunch included. I wanted more time with her. Actually I made her three different lunch and movie tickets. I wanted to be with her a lot!

I distinctly remember being in EMDR therapy, working through what turned out to be my last issue with the way my mom handled things, when it dawned on me.

I had forgiven the boys. Now I was ready to forgive my mom for forgetting what happened to me. She must have had her reasons. Maybe she couldn't cope with the painful emotions and boxed the whole thing up just like I did. It didn't matter anymore. The Lord helped me let it go!

Finally, finally, I was free. And so was she.

> *Lord, wow, forgiveness feels so good!*
> *Thank You for making the impossible possible.*
> *Because of You, there is a HUGE connection*
> *between forgiveness and joy.*

As my head began to heal—and it did, thanks be to God! Despite my doubts, my head injury healed completely and I had ice cream for lunch the day I got to break up with my concussion specialist, twenty-one weeks later than the ER docs predicted—and my need for PT and acupuncture appointments began to dwindle, we were both feeling sad. We were really used to having in-person time to connect, and we loved it.

I never thought I'd see the day.

So, when my concussion symptoms resolved completely and I "graduated" from the months of appointments, I asked my mom if we could have a standing weekly date. She said yes!

Ever since, we've gone on aimless adventures—with me as the driver. We've had dinner out, we've had dinner in. We've talked and laughed and shared.

We've continued to strengthen our connection.

God is so, so good. Let this serve as a testimony to the truth in Romans 8:28 about how He can use all things for good (see chapter 6). He used my head injury to give me one of the greatest blessings of my life: He gave me the relationship I always wanted to have with my mom. Because of this, I wanted to call this book *Why My Head Injury Was the Best Thing That Ever Happened to Me.*

Messy Joy fit on the cover better.

Messy Joy Spill-Your-Guts Journal Questions:

1. What are your thoughts about truly forgiving others who have hurt you? What does the Bible say about it?
2. Write about a time you forgave someone who did you wrong. How did forgiveness make you feel? What effect did it have on the amount of joy in your life?
3. Whom do you need to forgive?
4. Write a prayer asking the Lord to help you forgive the person who came to mind above.
5. Have you ever felt in bondage because you can't forgive someone? Write about your situation.
6. Where are you at emotionally: in the deep end, the shallow end, or somewhere in the middle? How has this served you? How has this held you back?
7. How connected are you with your family members? As you read this chapter, what came up for you regarding your connections?
8. If you've ever felt like a misfit, share what may have contributed to your feelings. How have you coped? How have you healed? What healing needs to take place?
9. How comfortable are you with your own level of emotional depth?
10. Are you able to talk with your family members about the things that matter most to you? Whom do you feel safest sharing your emotions with?

11. Our words have great power. When have you regretted the way your words came out and caused someone pain? What can be learned? Have you apologized?

12. Have you ever avoided someone because of your own need to heal from pain? How did this work out for you? What did you learn? If you could go back and do it again, would you do anything differently?

13. Share an example of a time God has used a big mess to bring great joy. What did you learn about yourself? About God? About joy?

CHAPTER 14

If You Add Joy to Your Mess, Will It Still Be Messy?

Yes.

Yay!

I could end this last chapter right there. I could celebrate finishing this crazy book with a Bruno Mars dance party and a family dinner served on china. Maybe a little "24K Magic" with homemade sundried tomato and bacon alfredo pizza on whole grain crust. With mushrooms and extra parmesan. Woohoo!

Not that I've been thinking about it or anything.

But wait, there's more.

If you act now, we'll also throw in this little gem . . .

I care too much about you to dance off into the purple-and-orange sunset without asking this question: do you see messy as a bad thing?

Seriously. Pause. Take a breath. What does your gut say? What's your view of messy?

Is messy negative?

Something that needs to be changed? Cleaned up? Improved?

If so, I can understand why you'd think messy and joy can't go together.

Joy is good, messy is bad, right?

In general, I would say most people agree. The title *Messy Joy* was intentionally chosen because these are words that don't usually play nicely together.

Messy and joy.

I wanted to get your attention. I needed you to pick this thing up and read it.

And now that we are getting to the end, I have to confess one final thing.

Are you ready? Here we go: I have a different view of messy.

Mmm hmm.

Wow. Just when you think you know someone.

Perspective is everything. How we view things can determine our actions—and our results. Here's an example. Every day, Molly loses a ball in the yard. She is obsessed with chasing balls, but sometimes my aim isn't accurate, and they end up lost.

Okay, every day, I lose a ball in the yard.

So the search begins. We know where I threw it, and we look right there. It's gone. We both search high and low, but the thing has disappeared into thin air. I could give up (and admittedly, sometimes I do). Or I could come at the search from another direction and change my perspective. So I look at it differently. Now I can see the same bush from another angle. And gosh dang it, either the bush rearranges itself when I'm not looking, or the new perspective makes that ball pop out of hiding and into plain sight.

And Molly is happy, and my throw is crappy, and we do it all over again.

So, when it comes to messy, I'll share my perspective. I'll throw it out there knowing that you are on the last chapter and unless you started reading in the back like my sweet friend Danice, you've read enough to know that I am not only a "glass is half full" girl, but I am also a "thank God the glass exists at all" kind of girl, and you'll expect that to shape my perspective.

If you come to my funeral, please make sure someone says that part about being thankful for the glass. Or just stand up and yell, "Robin was thankful the glass existed!" That would be a fun moment. And then make sure they play "We Need a Little Christmas" by Percy Faith and His Orchestra. It needs to be the really cheesy version that will make Rick, Missy, and Robbie roll their eyes, remembering all the times I insisted we play it and, when they complained it was dumb, had to listen to me say, "If I die tomorrow, won't you be glad we played this song?" Isn't a positive perspective great?

Okay, it's true, yes, I have a different view of messy and here it is: messy is good.

Messy is very, very good.

Now do you want me to end the book?

Yes, my friend, I am going to see the good in messy. And the good news is, you can too.

I can't help it: seeing the good runs deep. For some reason, I once won an award as the Dietetic Intern of the Year for our state. The "prize" was getting to present my nutrition case study to hundreds of experienced dietitians at this huge conference.

After shaking in my boots during my speech, my internship director said, "Only you could see the good in pancreatic cancer and make that story fun."

So, here we go: let's dig into it and find the good. If it feels good to feel good, and the concepts of messy and feeling good don't seem to go together, how can messy lives be good?

You know why our lives are messy in the first place? **Simply put, our lives are messy because we woke up on this side of the grass.**

Yup.

And that is a very good thing.

Isn't that amazing, folks? You're alive! How much would you pay for life? You won't see this in stores. Today only, you get the whole thing for thirty-nine low payments of $2.99 plus $65 shipping and handling. What a deal!

Seriously, messy lives are beautiful. They're dynamic. They're only possible because we are alive.

It's true.

If you want a life that's nice and neat, cleaned up and tidy and maybe even perfect (say it isn't so, not even my type As!), oh, you'll get it. The way I see it, just love Jesus and you'll get it in heaven.

In the meantime, I say, live this life and bring on the mess.

After all, dirty kids are happy kids.

Why would we buy into the belief that messy lives need to be changed when they are filled with amazing blessings:

- Challenge
- Grit

- Determination
- Trust and obedience
- Curiosity
- Learning
- Personal growth
- Perseverance
- Overcoming obstacles
- Recovery stories
- The blur of activity
- Purpose
- Adventure
- Spontaneity
- Relationships
- Stretched comfort zones
- Emotion
- Discoveries
- Wonder
- Excitement

You know where I'm going with this . . . joy. Messy lives can be filled with joy.

Read that again: messy lives can be filled with JOY!

I cannot contain my tears as I type. My friend, we should—in fact, we *get* to—live messy lives, and we get to embrace messy joy.

Holy cow.
Thank You, God!
It's amazing how messy joy can be a good thing.
Only You can surprise us like that.
You are just that cool!

I know I'm feeling kind of loopy, high on life and stuff, finishing a book I never wanted to start, celebrating the ways God met me in the pain and offered me joy instead. You might not be there yet. That's all right.

Need a little more convincing that we should embrace and not try to change messy joy? Maybe this exercise will be helpful.

When you think back to your most joy-filled times, imagine they are scenes from a movie of your life story. Take a moment and go there. What are the top three scenes?

Hmm . . .

Now, this movie is a blockbuster and some good-looking superstar plays the lead role of you.

What a hottie!

As you watch thirty minutes of movie trailers and subliminal ads for the concession stand, you're sitting in one of those sweet recliner seats. You've got popcorn. It's salty and has just the right amount of butter. You pour in the M&M's because you're a rebel like that.

The lights go down and the show starts.

What do you see? What do you remember?

What were the best parts of your life, up there on screen?

Take a minute to jot down the scenes in your journal (you'll see this question below, number 9). For real.

Wait, this book has journal questions?
But, like, are there any nachos left?

Now imagine you're holding the movie camera, and you can zoom out as you watch the scenes. Because this is your life story, you have the ability to pull back a little and see the bigger picture. You are seeing more than the significant joy-filled moments on the screen. This is where it gets interesting. Now you can see the fringy stuff, the parts that contributed to the best memories, the events that were happening at the same time as the good stuff.

My question for you is, what else are you seeing that has been hidden in the shadows of your brighter memories, almost forgotten, but was just as real, just as important?

Yes, even in our life's most precious experiences, in our greatest joys, if we look hard enough and allow ourselves to admit they existed, we'll discover that messes were also present.

Even our most amazing experiences were never actually perfect.

In fact, some of our favorite moments were only possible *because* of messes.

Would you ditch those messes knowing that their corresponding joys would also disappear? Of course not.

The messes made the joys more beautiful.

Mic drop.
Well, camera drop.

At first it might be tough to spot the messes because the truth is, we'd really prefer to remember the "positive" experiences. And that's okay. But if we look back and believe that life was perfect, we're doing ourselves a disservice.

When we take the time to think back and consider all that we've experienced—and I do mean *all*—we'll find that messy joy has been present in our lives all along . . . because we have been living. And that is what makes messy joy good.

If that didn't resonate today, give yourself grace. And space. Let it settle for a while. Make a note in your calendar to pick this chapter back up at another date (maybe it can be your recess break). See if time changes your perspective at all. In the meantime, perhaps some of these messy joy experiences will sound familiar:

- You marry the person of your dreams . . . and discover he or she snores like a wild banshee.
- You get so caught up in the excitement of opening Christmas presents . . . that the cinnamon rolls burn.
- You bring the baby you've prayed for home from the hospital . . . and say good-bye to free time and expendable cash as you know it for eighteen years. Or more.
- You do the happy dance when you get accepted into your top college choice . . . and then do nothing but work your tush off for four years straight.
- You land the perfect job . . . only to realize your boss never actually developed the skill set needed to be promoted above your entry level position.
- You buy a new house, a place of your very own . . . and discover that it's an endless money pit.
- You add an adorable pet to your family . . . and become a slave to cleaning up hair, puke, and poop.
- You have fun laughing and goofing around with your friends . . . and get attacked by a bunch of boys.
- You enjoy the freedom of wonderful, long walks . . . and end up with a debilitating foot condition.
- You savor the taste of delicious macaroni and cheese and brownies . . . and screw up your gut health.
- You go on an adventure with your favorite people on the planet . . . and come home with a head injury.

The list goes on and on. And isn't it wonderful? Each messy joy experience we have brings with it the opportunity to become more resilient.

Resilience, much like joy, is contagious. When you have it, you can't help but want others to have it too. Happiness feels good, but it doesn't bring resilience. It brings a cycle of ups and downs, leading to a continual state of wanting.

But when you've cultivated joy that lasts even when things are tough, before long you're pouring encouragement into people who are struggling, saying just the thing they needed to hear. It's the stuff so tough we would rarely sign up willingly for again that teaches us the most and allows us to be the most of service to others in need.

I am reminded of these verses:

> **"We are troubled on every side, yet not distressed;**
> **we are perplexed, but not in despair; Persecuted,**
> **but not forsaken; cast down, but not destroyed."**
> *(2 Corinthians 4:8–9 KJV)*

> **"Praise be to the God and Father of our Lord Jesus Christ,**
> **the Father of compassion and the God of all comfort, who comforts**
> **us in all our troubles, so that we can comfort those in any trouble**
> **with the comfort we ourselves receive from God."**
> *(2 Corinthians 1:3–4)*

Resilience allows us to spread joy to the world.

I wonder what would happen if we tossed out the idea of living perfect lives on this side of heaven and instead embraced the fulfillment that comes with living lives filled with messy joy because they perfectly position us to share our lessons of perseverance with others? That's probably the longest sentence at the end of an even longer book, so here's a quick summary:

Ditch perfection —> Embrace messy joy —> Share the love

And while we're in "I wonder" mode . . . I wonder what would happen if we acknowledged joy when it popped up naturally and chose it intentionally when it didn't . . . even when the circumstances might stink. And what if we taught others to do the same? What would that world feel like?

I wonder what the headlines would read.

The other day, I was in a store, and I saw the cutest "Choose Joy" sign. If you've been living outside a cave at all these past few years, especially once the pandemic kicked in, you've seen "Choose Joy" plastered on mugs. Laptop stickers. Serving trays.

If it were up to me, it would also be on Band-Aids. Unemployment websites. Construction barrels. Clinic room walls. DMV check-in stations. Prison bars. Coffins.

The day I saw that "Choose Joy" sign, I was in a good place emotionally. I was excited to see it and wanted to buy several to give away.

But I remembered back to one of my lower moments, when I was still having PTSD nightmares and fearing my head injury wasn't going to heal, unable to eat away the pain with sugar and salt like I wanted to. The "Choose Joy" post I saw on social media landed a whole lot differently that day. I sort of wanted to smack the person who posted it. Sort of.

It's a matter of perspective, is it not?

On that day when I was feeling sorry for myself, I scoffed and thought, "Choose joy. I'm trying, but what right do I have? My life's a train wreck. I'm a joy coach living a secret nightmare. I'm a fraud. I should go become a store greeter."

Shout-out to store greeters everywhere.
I really do want to join your ranks.
Getting paid for smiling, chatting, and secretly
reorganizing the shelves when no one's looking
is the ultimate gig. Save me a spot.

And that's when it dawned on me. It was because I was entrenched in hurt, *because* my life was messy and I still wanted joy to be a reality anyway . . . these were the reasons I should not only keep choosing joy but continue encouraging others to choose it also. God was using it all to equip me to be the joy coach who walked the walk and talked the talk. My messy life didn't make me a fraud; it made me an expert.

And so does yours.

There is a world who needs to know how to choose joy. One quick scan of the headlines will confirm just how much we are hurting both collectively and individually.

We are expertly equipped and perfectly positioned to tell our tales and share our skills. When you meet someone who is struggling to believe that joy is possible because of the situation they are in, remind them that no life is beyond reach. If they truly want to know how to go beyond buying the trendy "Choose Joy" items and make it a reality, share these steps with them.

- First of all, if mental illness or unresolved pain is present, seek healing with the help of a professional therapist or counselor.
- Allow for space to consider what joy actually is, by your definition. Know what to put in your GPS so you have a clear destination.
- Think about how joy makes you feel physically . . . what happens? Does your heart beat differently? Do you feel lighter? Taller? Bouncier? Fuller? Does it affect your breathing? Are your knees tingly? Get specific.
- Make a Joy Bucket List of the things that light you up personally. It's okay if it's hard at first; things will come to you. For inspiration, remember back to times when you felt joy and what was taking place.
- Add to your list as things come up, as you feel joy in your body, and as you are thinking about joy more and more.
- Remain mindful of what's on your list. Post it somewhere visible to you every day, or even take a photo of it and make it the lock screen on your phone so you see it every time it lights up.

- Tell other people about your Joy Bucket List, and ask what's on theirs. It's fun to share because joy is so contagious. Speak of it often and encourage others to do the same. Sharing stories of times you've found joy in the trenches and the things that spark joy in you will breed more joy in each of you.

- Until Google cancels me for disagreeing with their definition of joy and wipes all trace of me off the internet, join my private group on Facebook, The Joy Bucket. That's where we keep the conversation going on a regular basis and encourage each other to seek and share joy.

- Ask yourself if you are making time for the things on your list so joy is a part of regular life, not just a response to crisis. Then, in a crisis situation, your experience with joy will come in especially handy.

- Check your calendar and find a time that you can reliably honor your decision to choose joy and feel good often. Think of it as a scheduled part of your day, something that happens no matter what.

- Go for it, make it happen, do things on your Joy Bucket List, and feel good without guilt. Change things up whenever you need to. Feeling joy will fill your joy bucket, and full buckets overflow. Yay! This is all about you feeling great and having more to give from when others are in need.

- Remember that being spontaneous can be a rich source of joy, so get out of your comfort zone by breaking free from your calendar and your to-do list for unplanned moments of joy. It's great to deviate, even in tiny ways.

Wow, I don't know about you, but the thought of embracing and sharing messy joy with a world in need fills my heart with purpose and makes me want to skip.

Joy tip: it's impossible to skip for sixty seconds
without smiling at least once. Try it, or imagine it.
How does it make you feel?

Life on this side of the grass isn't perfect for anyone. It's banged up, broken down, and full of surprises. And that's great because experiencing messes will make experiencing joys that much more amazing.

Bring on the potholes. God will meet you there to offer you joy even when you're swerving around banana peels and filled to overflowing with head trash with your "Choose Joy" T-shirt on.

During the ups and the downs of life, it feels good to feel good. Feel good. And always, always give your joy away to a world in need. It will multiply. Think fish and loaves.

So yes, my dear friend, if you add joy to your mess, it will still be messy. Yay! This means you're alive. Thankfully, because God is good (all the time), we get to embrace this gift called messy joy.

Let's break out the china and crank up the Bruno. It's time to celebrate!

"This is the day which the Lord hath made;
we will rejoice and be glad in it."
(Psalm 118:24 KJV)

Messy Joy Spill-Your-Guts Journal Questions:

1. What's your perspective: Do you see messy as a bad thing? A good thing? A mixture? Elaborate.
2. What's your view of how messy and joy go together?
3. Can you think of a time you changed your perspective and things worked out for the better?
4. What are some things you've seen the good in that people didn't expect?
5. How can your messy life be good?
6. What blessings are contained within your messy life?
7. What's your view of messy joy? Is it possible? Something to be embraced or avoided? Why?
8. Going back to a question from earlier in this book, do you believe life needs to be perfect and cleaned up before you can have joy?
9. As you thought about the joy-filled scenes of your life story on the big screen, what were the highlights?
10. As you mentally zoomed out of your life story, what messes did you see on the edges of the happy scenes?
11. Do you know someone who seems to have a nearly perfect life? What messes are part of that person's story?
12. What happened in your life that you would add to the list of the messy joy experiences supporting the "we need to embrace messy joy because it leads to resilience" message?

13. In general, do you feel you are as resilient as you'd like to be? Explain.

14. How do you acknowledge joy when it pops up naturally?

15. When it comes to choosing joy, how skilled are you?

16. How might you strengthen your joy-choosing skills? What area(s) do you need to focus on?

17. When you hear "choose joy," what comes up for you?

18. Do you feel more qualified and equipped to choose joy than you were before reading this book? To encourage others to choose it? Share your thoughts here.

19. Which items in the steps of how to choose joy jump out at you the most? Why?

20. What now is your personal definition of joy?

21. How does joy appear within your body? How do you feel it?

22. At this point, is it difficult or easy to add to your Joy Bucket List? How often are you thinking about it?

23. Have you posted your Joy Bucket List anywhere special? Where?

24. When you have discussed the things that bring you joy with others, where did the conversations go? How did they make you feel?

25. When you shared stories of times you've found joy in the trenches, what effect did it have on you? On the other person?

26. Do you feel you are making enough time for joy? If something needs to be adjusted, what's one easy step in that direction?

27. Write about a time your experience with joy came in handy during a crisis situation. What happened? What difference did choosing joy make?

28. Name three things that brought you joy today. Were they planned or spontaneous?

29. How do you feel about the level of joy in our world? Would sharing your joy make any difference? Can you name a time when you were in need and someone shared their joy with you?

30. Can you think of someone with an imperfect life who would benefit from embracing messy joy? If you'd like to help them, what steps can you take?

31. Is there anything you'd like me to know about your story? About the amount of joy in your life? About your experience with this book? If so, please do two things: leave a review for this book on Amazon, and then write to me, Robin, at Robin@joytotheworldcoaching.com.

ABOUT THE AUTHOR

ROBIN SHEAR is a joy coach, speaker, and founder of Joy to the World Coaching. She provides virtual joy coaching to givers who find themselves depleted. She has spent decades helping health care professionals, educators, and parents feel good so they can give from a place of fullness and lead effectively again. Through fun, customized coaching, Robin aids her clients in thinking optimistically, helps them define and incorporate joy into all aspects of their lives, and encourages them to share their joy with the world. She can help clients infuse joy into their family, love life, health and fitness, career, social life, spirituality, and sense of adventure, among other areas.

Robin is a Whole Person Certified Life Coach through the International Coaching Federation (ACC). Her blog, Joy Bites, on joytotheworldcoaching.com, helps readers reframe their thinking in a joyful direction. Just for the fun of it, she shares off-the-cuff "Robin Shear, One Take on Joy" videos on YouTube. Robin is the administrator of The Joy Bucket, a private group on Facebook that encourages members from around the world to share what brings them joy as a means of making joy more contagious than any virus.

Robin offers fun and engaging presentations to groups, with her signature presentation being "A Quick Hit of Joy: How to #Feelgood Fast." Attendees often declare they have never laughed that much at a conference, and they walk away inspired to take action that will enrich their lives. Several audience testimonials are found on her website.

Robin has served in various professional roles, including registered dietitian specializing in eating disorder treatment, youth director/pastor and developer of two vibrant youth programs, and life enrichment team member at senior living communities, two of which were memory care facilities. She found that joyful living was the common denominator that improved life for each of these populations. Robin's greatest sources of joy include making memories with her family, developing her Christian faith and learning about other faith traditions, connecting with people, being spontaneous, and helping others live fulfilling, rewarding lives.

She is a member of the International Coaching Federation and the Advanced Writers and Speakers Association. She was designated as a Global Presence Ambassador by Parenting 2.0, an international consciousness movement that promotes proactive education for life skills. Robin is frequently a featured expert in media stories and on podcasts and radio shows. She has been quoted in *TIME Magazine* and *The Wall Street Journal*, among other outlets. She loves to get her hands dirty and has volunteered with The Special Olympics, Habitat for Humanity, Compassion International, and Amigos for Christ. She and her husband have two adult children who both got married in 2022, plus their goldendoodle who likes to get on camera and steal the show.

Robin wants you to have joy and to have it now! To chat with her, send an email to robin@joytotheworldcoaching.com. She asks each reader to leave an Amazon review for this book so that the Messy Joy movement can be shared around the globe.

Reader Resources
- Joy to the World Coaching website: joytotheworldcoaching.com
- Joy Bites newsletter: joytotheworldcoaching.com/joybitesnewsletter
- 10 Unexpected JOYS (a starter list of things that may add joy to your life):joytotheworldcoaching.com/joylist

- 17 Questions: Connect and Find Joy (conversation starters that can help you feel the joy of connection in a hurry): joytotheworldcoaching.com/17questions
- "Are You Headed for Burnout?" Quiz: joytotheworldcoaching.com/quiz

Joy

BUCKET LIST

I find joy in:

_____

_____

_____

_____

_____

_____

_____

_____

_____

Joy Bucket List, continued

_____

_____

_____

_____

_____

_____

_____

_____

_____

_____

_____

_____

_____

_____

CPSIA information can be obtained
at www.ICGtesting.com
Printed in the USA
JSHW020344190123
36307JS00005B/17